The Future of Species

The Future of Species

THE FANTASY OF EVOLUTION -
THE SCIENCE OF CREATION

E. Roberts Alley

Unless otherwise indicated, Bible quotations are taken from *The English Standard Version of the Bible*, Copyright © 2001 by Crossway Bibles.
All rights reserved.

ISBN: 151714986X
ISBN 13: 9781517149864

Table of Contents

IF YOU HAVE AN INTEREST in history, or wonder why the subtitle of this book calls evolution *fantasy* and creation *science*, you might be most interested in the chapters in Book 1—The Past. If you have a concern about the present state of civilization or about US society in particular, please look at the chapters under Book 2—The Present in the Table of Contents. If your attention is most focused on the future, Book 3 addresses those issues.

Dedication ·xi
Foreword · xiii
    Introduction · xiii
    The Need for This Book · xiii
    Society's Need for Evolution ·xiv
    The Biblical Response to Society's Need · · · · · · · · · · · xv
    Science's Lack of Response to Society's Need · · · · · · · xv
    Theology's Lack of Response to Society's Need · · · · ·xvi
    How Should We Respond to Society's Need? · · · · · · ·xvii
    Darwin Enters the Picture ·xix
    Our Governments Enter the Picture · · · · · · · · · · · · · · · xx
    The Answer to Darwin, Science, and the
    Governments ·xxi
Preface · xxv
    The Power of Science through Evolution · · · · · · · · · · xxv
    The Power of Control through Evolution · · · · · · · · xxvii
    An Invitation to Think Critically · · · · · · · · · · · · · · ·xxviii

Book 1	The Past	1
Part 1	The Burden of Biases	3
Chapter 1	Introduction	5
	Going Forward into the Following Chapters	6
Chapter 2	Reasoning Past Biases	8
	Reasoning and Science	8
	The Human Condition	9
	The Human Response	10
	The Human Limitations	10
	The Question Remains	11
Chapter 3	The Problem of Existence	13
Chapter 4	Natural Reality	15
	The Natural Permanence of Nonliving Matter	16
	The Natural Death of Living Matter	17
Chapter 5	Do We Accept a Supernatural Reality?	19
Chapter 6	Beliefs	23
	Atheism	23
	Theistic Evolution	25
	Intelligent Design	26
	Judaism	26
	Christianity	27
Chapter 7	The Belief Documents	30
	Creation	30
	The Holy Bible	30
	Nature	35
	Evolution	36
	Introduction	36
	The Origin of Species, Charles Darwin[4]	36
	Genesis: The Scientific Quest for Life's Origin, Robert Hazen[5]	37
	The Future of Mankind, Pierre Teilhard[6]	38
	God and the New Physics, Paul Davies[7]	40

Part 2	The Origin through Creation	43
Chapter 8	Introduction	45
Chapter 9	The Beginning of Supernatural Reality	47
Chapter 10	Day One of Creation, the Earth	51
Chapter 11	Day Two of Creation, the Sky	56
Chapter 12	Day Three of Creation, Vegetation	58
Chapter 13	Day Four of Creation, the Universe and Time	62
Chapter 14	Day Five of Creation, Aquatic Life and Birds	67
Chapter 15	Day Six of Creation, Animals and Humans	70
	Summary of Creation	73
Part 3	The Origin through Evolution	77
Chapter 16	Introduction	79
Chapter 17	The Beginning of Natural Reality	81
	The Big Bang Theory	82
	The Center of the Universe	84
	The Origin of the Universe	85
	The Distance to Stars	86
	The High Temperature of the Early Earth	87
	Geological Age	87
	The Age of the Universe	88
	Dust on the Moon	88
	Radiocarbon Dating	89
	Radioisotope Dating	90
	Biblical Dating of the Universe	90
Chapter 18	Chemical Changes, Inorganic to Organic	92
Chapter 19	Chemical Changes, Organic to Living Vegetative Organic	95
Chapter 20	Chemical Changes, Living Vegetative Organic to Living Animal Organic	98
	Locomotion	101
	Sight	102
	Flight	103
	Genetics	103

Chapter 21	Chemical Changes, Living Animal Organic to Humans	107
	Dinosaurs Preceded Humans	109
	The Missing Links	110
Book 2	The Present	113
Chapter 22	Introduction	115
Chapter 23	The State of Inorganics and Organics	117
	Introduction	117
	Inorganics	117
	Organics	118
	Air Pollution	118
	Carbon Dioxide as a Pollutant	119
	Global Warming	122
	Climate Change	125
	Water Pollution	126
	Land Pollution	128
Chapter 24	The State of Humans, the Christian View	130
	Summary	139
Chapter 25	The State of Humans, the Secular View	140
	The State of Our Society	140
Chapter 26	Finding Myself	142
Chapter 27	Reinventing Myself	144
Chapter 28	The Solution for our Present State	146
Chapter 29	The Re-Creation of the New World	148
	The Need for a New World	148
Book 3	The Future	153
Part 1	The Future through God	155
Chapter 30	Introduction	157
Chapter 31	Oneness with God	160
Chapter 32	The New Heaven and New Earth	163
Chapter 33	The Alternative to Heaven	169
Chapter 34	The Interim Future of Species	173
	Our Interim Needs	175
	Should We Agree to Disagree?	177

	Will We Be Liberal or Conservative?	178
	The End Times	180
Part 2	**The Future through Evolution**	183
Chapter 35	**Introduction**	185
Chapter 36	**The Omega Point**	187
Chapter 37	**Reliance on Science as We Move into the Future**	189
Chapter 38	**Can Our Art and Science Advance?**	191
Part 3	**How We Can Affect the Future**	193
Chapter 39	**The Future of Wealth, Jobs, and Education**	195
	Wealth Accumulation or Distribution	195
	Jobs	197
	Taxes	200
	Education	201
	Summary	203
Chapter 40	**The Future of Racial Relations**	205
Chapter 41	**The Future of Marriage and Families**	207
	Marriage	207
	Sexual Variants	208
	Divorce	213
	Families	213
Chapter 42	**The Future of Health Care**	215
Chapter 43	**The Future of Social Life**	217
Chapter 44	**The Future of Retirement**	219
Chapter 45	**The Future of the Church**	222
Chapter 46	**Conclusion**	225
	Acknowledgments	233
	About the Author	235

Dedication

This book is dedicated to those of a wide variety of interests. The purpose of this book is to communicate with all readers, regardless of gender. In order to prevent awkwardness, I will use the masculine "he", intead of the feminine "she", or the neutral "their", when referring to humans, but the intent is to include both genders. The goal of this book is to challenge you to critically investigate the idea of a spiritual or supernatural reality. This unseen reality exceeds and controls the more obvious natural reality, which we all strive to understand and—in some cases—worship. So this book is dedicated to the following seekers:

To the *Christian* who in his naïveté, has believed the teaching and the indoctrination he has received from school, the media, and the government; who has attempted to balance the natural and spiritual realities in order to make them noncontradictory and of equal weight—but who is curious enough and bold enough to question his beliefs and those of his teachers.

To the *theologian* who has attempted to allow science and religion to coexist as equals; who has made the grievous mistake of teaching his followers that the Bible must conform to scientific theory to be true, that God has been confusing in His communication with His chosen people to the point that He has used allegory, myth, and literary framework to hide the obvious truths of His inspired words; who has, in his pride, assumed that his education, experience, position, or ordination has allowed him and his peers to be the only true interpreters of God's truth; who teaches that God has deliberately hidden truths in His plain words that are greater than can be understood by the uninitiated "priesthood of the saints"—but who is open to the acceptance of a deeper reality of humbly listening to God and His everlasting truths.

And to the serious *scientist* who, in his understanding of his field of expertise, has completely forgotten the more critical and permanent spiritual truths that supersede and govern natural theories, regardless of how intellectually impressive; who has let his arrogance and his respect and reverence for science degrade his logic and reason to the point that he is blinded to the greater spiritual truths of the presence of God with His omniscience, omnipresence, and omnipotence, a God Who has allowed His communication to His children to be perfectly understood without (or with) the benefit of special intensive education, membership, or intelligence—but who has the capacity and humility to realize that there could be a spiritual reality that he has no qualifications or experience to discern without God's help.

I dedicate this book to all of you—plus to those who may agree with some or all of my conclusions—to the praise of God, Jesus, and the Holy Spirit, Who we all are called to glorify and enjoy forever.

By the way, I have been in all of the categories above.

Foreword

When a blind beetle crawls over the surface of a curved branch, it doesn't notice that the track it has covered is indeed curved. I was lucky enough to notice what the beetle didn't notice. Albert Einstein, 1922, 8

INTRODUCTION
EACH CHAPTER OF THIS BOOK **begins with a quote from Albert Einstein, a Jewish scholar who was probably the most brilliant scientist of the twentieth century.**[1] **To me these quotes demonstrate that Einstein understood that evolution in its currently accepted state is a fantasy rather than a fact.** It is not my intent to show agreement with Einstein's specific statements, but to show how a very intelligent and confident scientist can reason through scientific pressures and discern the ultimate truth.

THE NEED FOR THIS BOOK
In my opinion there is a critical need today for someone to write a scientific and theological treatise to refute many of the conclusions that Charles Darwin reached in his *The Origin of Species*[2] and that his followers have extrapolated over the years—and to use the words of God in the

Bible, as well as true science, to analyze our current status and predict our future potential.

I have attempted to write this book not just as an opinion piece and, instead, have presented the facts from science and the Bible, as I understand them. In a very real way, all literature consists of opinion. My understanding of facts is just my opinion. An author cannot be completely opinion free, or he has nothing to add to the existing body of literature. For instance, all textbooks are the author's opinion of facts, and all fiction is opinion, as evidenced by the thoughts and actions of the characters. For this reason, I have included many quotes from the Bible and from prominent thinkers in the fields of creationism and evolution. Some of the more publicized pontificators, I have ignored because of shallow logic or limited experience.

Most of the world accepts the theory of evolution as science, rather than as an unproven theory. There seems to be no energy or desire to question the completely unproven statements in *National Geographic Magazine*, *Smithsonian Magazine*, *Nature Journal*, *Scientific American Magazine*, and newspapers that the universe is billions of years old, humans have been on this earth for millions of years, and that they evolved from apes. Scientifically, contrary to modern thought, the acceptance of evolution today is as outdated as the Flat Earth Society.

Society's Need for Evolution

Thousands of books have been written and billions of dollars spent promoting naturalism and the theory of evolution, as man desperately attempts to think himself into god. If we can explain our existence as a natural, accidental process, we don't need a God. We can be free from the rules of religion and can control our own lives and those of others. Not only can we be all-powerful, we can conveniently excuse the greed, selfishness, and hatred within us as simply the result of inheritance from nonthinking, amoral animals and vegetables.

The Origin of Species and the millions of pages promoting the theory of evolution have been written as a response to the approximately one thousand pages of the Bible and its Creation story, not visa versa. God finished His account of Creation in the Bible, and there is no real reason to go beyond that account with our imagination. **In a few pages, God conveyed a concise account of the beginning of the universe, explaining where and how it was formed, which has never been proven wrong in the thousands of years since it was written.**

Fundamentally, the argument between Creation and evolution is not between religion and science but between competing world views: supernaturalism versus naturalism.

The Biblical Response to Society's Need

Since evolution is a response to biblical creationism, this book will describe how God explained the origin of species and will then explore how those who do not accept the biblical account have responded. Likewise, this book will describe how God has provided for the future of species. And as a bridge between the two, we will look at the current condition of the species and the choices that we must face.

Science's Lack of Response to Society's Need

Charles Darwin popularized the ancient theory of evolution in *The Origin of Species* in 1859, and, since then, scientists, sociologists, philosophers, and teachers have used his theories as permission to go beyond his biological theories into bizarre imaginary and scientifically scandalous descriptions of historical life from nothing: spontaneous generation without creation.

In the last few years, scientists have been like Einstein's "blind beetles," not noticing the obvious presence of God in reality. I call for a freedom from tradition and an openness to the truth of God.

In my opinion, too few scientists have been bold enough and free enough from societal pressures to influence the communicators today—the teachers and the media—and to stand up for the laws of science by teaching theories as theories, rather than as science. The *2009 Pew Research Center Report*, Section 4, "Scientists, Politics, and Religion," states that 33 percent of scientists in the United States believe in God, 51 percent believe in a higher power, and 41 percent believe in neither. The highest percentage believing in God were the youngest, ages eighteen to thirty-four (42 percent). The poll also reported that 41 percent of chemists believe in God, but only 29 percent of astronomers do. This contrasts with 95 percent of all people polled believing in a higher power and 83 percent believing in God. In 2014, Elaine Howard Ecklund, of Rice University—who was sponsored by The American Association for the Advancement of Science, which also sponsored the Pew Poll—polled ten thousand people in the United States and found that 79.9 percent believe in God, 73.6 percent were Christian, and 15.5 percent were atheists, agnostics, or of no religion. This poll found 73.9 percent of scientists were believers in God, 61.1 percent were Christian, and 24.4 percent were atheists, agnostics, or of no religion.

These numbers conflict with the Pew poll, which usually indicates that questions were unclear or biased in one poll or the other. In either case, the number of scientists who are Christian are obviously not making much noise and are allowing the unbelievers to be the influencers. Another interesting statistic from the Pew Report is that of all Nobel Prize Laureates between 1901 and 2000, 67 percent believed in God. Comparable polls taken eighty years apart did not differ significantly in the percentage of scientist who identified as believers.

THEOLOGY'S LACK OF RESPONSE TO SOCIETY'S NEED

Fewer and fewer theologians have had the courage in recent years to teach the hundreds of verses in the Bible that describe Creation by God as a spiritual fact—a miracle no greater than other less controversial miracles such as the virgin birth, the resurrection of the dead, and the existence of a spiritual heaven and hell. They have instead bowed to the god of science and have explained scripture in a way that will match their understanding of science, or the understanding of others who are more qualified in their minds.

God has revealed, and continues to reveal, Himself in two ways: natural revelation through His Creation and special revelation through His written Word. He cannot be right in one and wrong in the other. If there is a contradiction, it is because we understand one or both records wrongly.

How Should We Respond to Society's Need?

We stand at a crossroad of paths to choose. One choice is to follow the dark delusion of Darwin toward a future of terrorism, crime, war, and a destruction of science. The second choice is an acceptance of the reality of the supernatural and of an omnipresent God. This path will lead toward morality, peace, and a return to the scientific and religious enlightenment for which we have the potential. If you have doubts at this point, see the references to Hitler and Marx below in the Preface.

The purpose of this book is to examine both the theories of evolution and the theory of Creation from a scientific perspective and from a spiritual or supernatural perspective. It is also to encourage the reader to decide which theory is true and which will lead us to a better future.

There has been much effort recently to convince us that religion and science can coexist. This can only be true if the religious will listen to and respect scientists, but not worship them or believe that everything they say is necessarily true. And it can only be true if the scientists will listen to and respect the religious, and try to answer the difficult question of the possible existence of a supernatural reality. Without this recognition of a spiritual world, scientists will never understand Creation, and coexistence of religion and science will be nothing more than a compromise that misses the real truth.

I grew up being taught, as many of us were, theistic evolution. That teaching, especially in the educational systems of the world today, has morphed into an atheistic, secular evolution—a theory that Darwin did not teach or believe.[3]

We need to pause and ask why our government, our media, and our schools are forcing a belief in one theory (evolution) while prohibiting the acceptance, or even study, of another theory (creationism). As a result of this indoctrination effort, it is considered more sophisticated and intellectual today to take the word of a minority of our scientists rather than the word of the spiritual God. Where is academic freedom? It is nonexistent for the supernaturalist.

A student in my Sunday-school class challenged me by asking me what theory of the development of man I believed. I admitted that I was a theistic evolutionist, believing that God created the world with its plants and animals, and when animals had developed to a certain level, God provided the animals with a mind that would enable them to rule the world. I was not far from Darwin's belief in life being "breathed into a few forms or into one."[4] In order to meet the student's challenge, I spent a week researching literature to confirm my evolutionary belief. I returned to Sunday school the next week, having completely changed my mind, and since then I have been a creationist.

This was about 1976, three years after I had received my master of science degree in environmental engineering, and I am ashamed to say that my change in belief was primarily scientifically based, rather than faith based. My education and my career in the almost forty years since, have both been in protecting and preserving the environment in the air, the water, and the land. These realms, along with living organisms in each of the realms—the only things, either evolved or created, that support the "species."

Since that fateful experience in Sunday school, the challenge I faced has become a challenge to learn more and to communicate to others why

I believe that Darwin produced a book of limited scope that was scientifically indefensible—except in his conclusions on microevolution of botany and biology. His peers led him, in his meager education and experience, to promote a theory that is much broader in scope than his research demonstrated. I have spent much more time since 1976 studying and researching the latest publications that deal with both evolution and creationism. This effort has confirmed my rather hasty conclusions of long ago, rather than resulting in a return to my previous more comfortable and more acceptable position.

Darwin Enters the Picture

When Darwin published *The Origin of Species* in 1859, the world was ripe for some excuse to remove God from societal thought.

"Darwin was never a model student but became a passionate amateur naturalist."[5] He was sent to Shrewbury School for an Anglican education in 1818 at the age of nine. His father considered him a "wastrel" and sent him to Edinburgh University in 1825 to study medicine.[6] He did not like medicine and became associated with some dissident students who were barred from graduating from Oxford and Cambridge, and he was introduced to the idea of a design for humanity that excluded the Divine.[7] His father reacted by sending him to Christ's College in 1827 to become an Anglican parson. Darwin finally received a bachelor of arts degree in 1831.[8] After this mediocre educational experience, Darwin spent five years on an around-the-world tour as a "self financed gentleman companion to the twenty-six-year-old captain" of the HMS Beagle to "investigate the geology and zoology of the lands he visited."[9]

Darwin set out the basic principle of eugenics (good breeding) in *The Descent of Man*:

> Thus the weak members of civilized societies propagate their kind. No one who has attended to the breeding of domestic animals will doubt that this must be highly injurious to the

race of man. It is surprising how soon a want of care, or care wrongly directed, leads to the degeneration of a domestic race; but excepting in the case of man himself, hardly anyone is so ignorant as to allow his worst animals to breed.[10]

Darwin's cousin, Francis Galton, later founded the eugenics movement, which Hitler adopted as justification for genocide.

Our Governments Enter the Picture

Today we are still blindly following Darwin's theory, and the scientists who support it, in order to continue to remove God from our government and our schools. Our thoughts today, even more so than in Darwin's day, are so tied up in the power of politics and the media that the "separation of church and state" has morphed into a separation of religion and state—which is considered constitutional—when this concept was simply a minority belief among our founders, accepted because of their traumatic history with England. But the Declaration of Independence clearly establishes the founders' belief in a creator ("endowed by their Creator"), and the Constitution clearly establishes the free exercise of religion in Amendment 1. More than ever, the leaders of our society today seem to have an urgent emotional need to remove God from all public thought. That is a logical goal for a humanist in power, since earthly power can control the natural order through education and government, but the humanist is powerless to control the supernatural order.

So governments have relegated spiritual faith to the "closet" and have prohibited its discussion in public in the belief that without exposure, an idea dies. Today then, it is critical to the future of Christianity, and indeed the future of our country, that freedom of speech and religion be returned. Those who have inquiring minds and are able to reason critically must speak out for our constitutional right to exercise our religion in public. For my part I have elected to concentrate on the questions raised as a result of the two theories of why we are here and what our future holds. These issues are important to me, since I believe there is a good future for many of us that encompasses freedom, but this future will not acquired through osmosis or even through our own efforts. I also accept that the future I will describe in this book is an extension of our past, including our creation.

THE ANSWER TO DARWIN, SCIENCE, AND THE GOVERNMENTS

Present societal practices warrant a response to *The Origin of Species* in order to demonstrate that even though evolution is an attractive theory, it does not explain the beginning of reality or time, the origin of matter, or the more important subjects of the supernatural and t*he future of species.*

Society has defined "religion" for us. Webster's defines it as "the service and worship of God and the supernatural." If God and the supernatural are myth, then that definition is legitimate, and religion should be treated as just another belief and practice, restricted to the supernatural. But if God is real, the supernatural has to be real, and that reality supersedes all natural reality in that it is more powerful, more knowledgeable, and is completely integrated into total reality as we experience it. So it is impossible to have a "separation" of the larger reality (supernatural) from the smaller (natural) reality; it is all from one source and all real. The belief in and *worship of God and the supernatural* is not only a belief, it is the truth—a truth that is recognized by 85 percent of the population of the world[11] and 92 percent of the US population.[12] Those religious people do also serve the natural, but they don't worship it. So a more realistic definition of "religion" is "the belief and faith in God."

It is irrational for members of the scientific community to call a religious faith a crutch or an illogical delusion when that community has no education, and perhaps no experience, in the supernatural or spiritual. They are unqualified and dishonest when they reach such a conclusion. **A spiritual belief is personal and very real, and no one—scientist or not—possesses the ability to judge that faith.**

Richard Dawkins in his book *The Greatest Show on Earth* states that deniers of evolutionary theory should be intellectually scorned and marginalized in the same way that Holocaust deniers should be. He said in a *New York Times* book review, "It is absolutely safe today to say that if you meet someone who claims not to believe in evolution, that person is ignorant, stupid, or insane (or wicked, but I'd rather not consider that)"[13]. How's that for sane scientific honesty?

It is an abuse of the right to free speech for a teacher, an administrator, or a politician to deny a student, a teacher, or a constituent the freedom to express his or her faith verbally, in prayer, or in written form—whether in school, on public property, or in media—regardless of the religion, unless the person is verbally abusing others. And disagreement is not abuse, regardless of a person's sensitivity.

I hope that the facts and theories presented in this book will convince readers that the future of species is settled, spiritually and naturally. **We have the answer to the question of our future; it is controlled by God, our Creator, through His finished plan for humankind toward a permanent existence with that Creator.**

If you are looking for a scientific answer to the question of the future of species, and not a spiritual one, you will be unsuccessful because history teaches us that science cannot predict the future accurately; only God can do that. And if you don't accept the existence of God, you will be forever frustrated by not being able to explain to yourself—or to anyone else—the origin of the building blocks of the universe and the supernatural occurrences that we experience continuously.

Evolution is a theory and not a scientific law since, in order to become law, a theory must be observed, documented, and reproducible by peers.

No other unproven scientific theory has ever been so widely accepted by society, to the extent that it is taught as science in schools all over the world. I call on all readers to critically examine the evidence presented in this book and elsewhere and to logically reach a conclusion before accepting unproven theories.

---

1 Alice Calaprice, *The New Quotable Einstein* (Princeton University Press, 2005). (All of the quotes in the chapter introductions are from this book.)
2 Charles Darwin, *The Origin of Species*, 1859 (New York, New York: Bantam Books, 1999).
3 Ibid. p399
4 Ibid. p 395,400
5 *Darwin Online: Biography*, Charles Darwin: Gentleman Naturalist, p3 of 26, accessed 10/05/15.
6 *Encyclopaedia Britannica*, Charles Darwin, British naturalist, p2 of 14, accessed October 5, 2015.
7 Ibid. p2 of 14
8 Ibid. p2 of 14
9 Ibid. p2 of 14
10 Charles Darwin and John Murray, *The Descent of Man and Selection in Relation to Sex* (Albemarle Street, 1871) 873.
11 "A Reason to Believe," Beth Azar, American Psychological Association, 2010.
12 "More than 9 in 10 Americans Continue to Believe in God," Frank Newport, Gallup, 2011.
13 "Darwin, Mind and Meaning," Alvin Plantinga and John A. O'Brien, University of Notre Dame, Virtual Library of Christian Philosophy, 1996, Calvin.edu.

Preface

I have not yet eaten enough of the Tree of Knowledge, though in my profession I am obliged to feed on it regularly. Albert Einstein, 1919, 5

I HAVE NOT YET EATEN enough of the Tree of Knowledge, though in my profession I am obliged to feed on it regularly. Albert Einstein, 1919, 5 As we study the deeply established societal belief in evolution, we must understand the full ramifications of the belief and the power it gives our scientists, educators, and politicians over our thoughts beliefs, and future.

THE POWER OF SCIENCE THROUGH EVOLUTION

The book *The Origin of Species* by Charles Darwin, first published in 1859, excited many scientists and others—who in the words of Pierre Teilhard de Chardin, "But to the minds of the majority our human condition seemed finally to be exalted by the fact that we were rooted in the fauna and soil of the planet-evolving Man in the forefront of the animals."[1] Teilhard understood exactly what Darwin was proposing: theistic evolution—a creation of one or more elementary organic compounds by God, which evolved over great periods of time into plants and animals and later into humans.

In recent years, most evolutionists have taken the liberty to extrapolate Darwin's theory, in their excitement of finding an excuse to eliminate God from science, into an as-yet unexplained and unproven theory that inorganic matter existed forever and somehow, miraculously, ordered itself into the very complex helix molecule DNA (deoxyribonucleic acid). It is true that Darwin did not understand the structure of DNA, but he said very clearly that "analogy would lead me one step further, namely, to the belief that all animals and plants have descended from some one prototype...probably all the organic beings which have ever lived on this earth have descended from some one primordial form, into which life was first breathed."[2]

In Darwin's world, science had a deep need to explain the existence of nature without, at that time, the popular belief that God created all things. If that popular belief were so, science would be limited and unable to explain the most important questions. Beginning in the Industrial Revolution, science was used to control popular thought, including the hope for a better future. If God created nature and continued to manipulate it, as so many believed, science would lose its preeminent position of authority and be relegated to mere mechanics.

That dire need evidenced in the middle of the nineteenth century survives in the scientific community today. **If science can explain why we are here and can control our future through scientific advancement, scientists will remain in their exalted position in society. But if supernaturalists return to the power they held in the nineteenth century, science will return to a secondary profession, and that is why scientists are so desperate to have the world accept the theory of evolution.**

In order to solidify their position, recent scientists have abandoned the laws of science and have begun to accept theory as science—instead of seeking understanding as opposed to control. They don't reach conclusions from the scientific results themselves but from philosophical premises.[3]

The Power of Control through Evolution

Wise people have always told me that when something is inexplicable, "look for the money." I have modified the adage to say, "look for the money and/or power." Well, scientifically, Darwin's microevolution doesn't pass the test as a scientific law—and it doesn't even make sense to a thinking layperson—but it does provide a means to control civilization.

Evolution was one of the sources of Hitler's dream of a master race and Karl Marx's dream of a socialist state, and today it is one of the sources of power in education and government around the world. If mankind has evolved from lower animals, only instinct and long-term heredity matter, and all human failure is explained by accidental evolution. In this case an individual would be helpless to avoid poverty, sickness, or depression, since evolutionary heredity would control all human conditions, actions, and reactions—just as it does in animals. There would be no standards of justice in educational or athletic success, grading, or awards, since people would not be responsible for themselves. Instead those who have less would be entitled to everything anyone else has through redistribution of wealth, comfort, health, food, clothing, shelter, and fame.

Darwin's book has survived over 150 years as a "scholarly text" to the point that it is almost considered a bible of humanism, but it doesn't address the future. I found several books with similar themes including: *The Future of Life* by E. O. Wilson; *The Future of Our Species* by A. Moore; *Voyage of Darwin's Beagle: On the Future of Species*; *The Future of Mankind*, a film documentary; *The Future of Humankind* by Von Abbot Hsuan Hue; and *The Future of Humankind* by Bertrand Russell. But none of these books addressed thr futurebof species from both a scientific and theological perspective.

Even though scientists have discarded most of Darwin's theories, including that of a Creator, his treatise remains the foundation of evolution as taught by law in most public-school systems of the world. It is very convenient in a secular society to adopt a theory that

allows the elimination of God from education, using the false pretext that Darwin explained that there is no need for God in evolution.

Darwin properly limited his observations to his areas of expertise: biology and, especially, botany. *The Origin of Species* has the reputation of being much broader in scope and to include the origin of the inorganic air, water, and land that support species. It is illogical to assume that the organic part of the universe is evolving, while the inorganic has always existed and has never evolved. Darwin never speaks of the origin of inorganics—nor do most evolutionary scientists, because they cannot. The only difference between inorganics and organics is that organics are all hydrocarbons. The only difference between living organics and nonliving organics, besides their complexity, is that nonliving organics have no DNA to program life; therefore, they cannot move on their own, grow, or reproduce.

An Invitation to Think Critically

Scientists are taught to think critically and to reason deductively, and that is what I will attempt to do in this book. Darwin reasoned inductively. In other words, he was influenced in his formulative years by men such as J. S. Henslow, a professor of botany at Cambridge University, astronomer Sir John Herschel, traveller Alexander von Humboldt and geologist Charles Lyell to believe in a new way of understanding nature through cumulative changes over immense periods of time that produced large changes. This unscientific preconceived conclusion is the reason Darwin failed.[4]

Astronomer Guillermo Gonzalez and philosopher/theologian Jay W. Richards conclude in their interesting book *The Privileged Planet* (Regnery Publishing, Inc. 2004) that "perhaps we have been staring past a cosmic signal far more significant than any mere sequence of numbers, a signal revealing a universe so skillfully crafted for life and discovery that it seems to whisper of an extraterrestrial intelligence immeasurably more vast, more ancient, and more magnificent than anything we've been willing to expect or imagine." Critical, open thinking can reveal truth, even in the face of scientific opposition and ridicule.

Wernher Von Braun, the leading scientist in the US space program, said, "One cannot be exposed to the law and order of the universe without concluding that there must be a design and purpose behind it all... To be forced to believe only one conclusion—that everything in the universe happened by chance—would violate the objectivity of science itself."[5]

Contrary to most evolutionary scientists (an oxymoron if there ever was one), one can be a believer in God and in His Creation, with or without natural critical thinking or any type of natural rational argument. A person can also be completely rational in believing in God and Creation. It is irrational scientifically to ignore the origin of matter and life, or the reason for organic death, or the presence of the supernatural, as does evolution. It is rational to consider faith in the supernatural. Remember that there is no scientific proof that there is no God or no Creation, just as there is none to prove that there is. Natural science or natural reasoning cannot address the existence of a supernatural being. So natural reasoning, as well as science, must stay within its bounds and be neutral to God—not antagonistic—to be critically honest.

Alvin Plantinga, who *Time* calls "America's leading orthodox Protestant philosopher of God," quotes John Stek in his *Conclusion of Methodological Naturalism*, Part 2:

> Theology must take into account of all that humanity comes to know about the world, and science must equally take into account of all that we come to know about God. **In fact, we cannot, without denying our being and vocation as stewards, pursue theology without bringing to that study all that we know about the world, nor can we, without denying our being and vocation as stewards, pursue science without bringing to that study all that we know about God** [3].

Dr. Stek was a professor of Old Testament at Calvin Theological Seminary and editor of the New International Version of the Bible.

In order to objectively explore the origin, the present, and the future of not only species, but the universe as it serves to support species, this book will contain three interrelated books: *The Past*, *The Present* and *The Future*, all describing the condition of species.

Eating from Einstein's "Tree of Knowledge" quoted above is, of course, the source of the Fall and, therefore, the curse on the world. The reason for the Fall was that Adam and Eve's decided to "be like God, knowing good and evil." If that is our goal in obtaining knowledge, we are forever lost. But if our goal is to understand nature and draw closer to understanding God, without replacing Him, then learning from the Tree of Knowledge of the Bible and from true science is a very noble pursuit.

I would suggest that the reader examine the Table of Contents of this book to see if any of the subjects covered are of interest. If so, the rest of the book can serve as background for the conclusions reached.

---

1 Pierre Teilhard de Chardin, *The Future of Mankind* (Harper & Row, 1959) chapter 22, 1 of 5, online.
2 Charles Darwin, *The Origin of Species*, 1859 (New York, NY: Bantam Books, 1999) 395,400
3 Alvin Plantinga, *Methodological Naturalism*, Calvin Virtual Library of Christian Philosophy, 1997. 9 of 17
4 John van Wyhe, *Darwin Online: Biography, Charles Darwin: Gentleman Naturalist*, accessed October 30, 2014, 3-5 of 26.
5 Dennis R. Petersen, *Unlocking the Mysteries of Creation* (Christian Equippers International, 1987), 335.

Book 1
The Past

Part 1
The Burden of Biases

CHAPTER 1

Introduction

*Imagination is more important than knowledge.
Knowledge is limited. Imagination encircles
the world. Albert Einstein, 1929, 9*

IN ORDER TO EXAMINE THE questions of the origin, evolution, present, and future of species, we must examine and admit our presuppositions and biases. If we inductively reason, as did Darwin and his followers, we start with a presupposition—and that bias affects our conclusion. We end up using cyclical reasoning in our desperate attempt to prove our bias. One could argue that creationists also use inductive reasoning, starting with the supposition that God's Word is true. But to a Christian, God's Word is law—even more so than scientific laws—since it is considered perfect. Unlike evolutionists, creationists should follow their law, while evolutionists are encouraged to break their scientific laws, or their reason will fail, as explained below.

These are some of the difficult questions we must ask in examining ourselves, if we truly desire to reach the truth, regardless of our present position:

- Do we consider that reality is limited to natural things, those we can discern with our five senses, or do we believe in a reality that consists of the natural and the supernatural?

- Have we taught or written about our beliefs in origins so that we are committed to a particular position that would be awkward or embarrassing to refute?
- Are we part of an organization or group that has an accepted belief of origins? If so, would we be allowed to state within that group a diverging viewpoint without being ostracized or censured?
- Have we been taught to—or do we naturally—reason inductively or deductively? Are we objective or subjective in our problem solving?
- Does our belief system have a document from which it operates (i.e., a constitution, bylaws, a mission statement, or other statement of belief and purpose)? If so, what is our assurance of the accuracy and permanency of that document?

Our presuppositions and biases will likely affect our objectivity in examining these issues. We should therefore be very cautious that we are completely rational in our thought process.

Einstein said, "Few people are capable of expressing with equanimity opinions that differ from the prejudices of their social environment. Most people are even incapable of forming such opinions."[1]

Going Forward into the Following Chapters

In order to compare the claims of evolution and Creation, I will refer to some of the documents accepted by the believers of the two theories. The believers in evolution accept a wide variety of documents, from *The Origin of Species* to scientific writings, books, and textbooks that have been written in the years since Darwin. This book will quote from some of these documents to compare the integrity of the theories.

Since this book invites readers to pick and choose the chapters that are of the most interest, I have necessarily repeated some conclusions in different chapters. I hope this is not distracting to those who choose to read the pages consecutively.

We will first discuss some basic and common biases and how they can be overcome. **Let us grow and learn with Einstein that the imagination of the supernatural is more important than the knowledge of the natural.**

---

1 Alice Calaprice, *The New Quotable Einstein*, , 2005, (Princeton, NJ: Princeton University Press),120

CHAPTER 2
Reasoning Past Biases

❦

As a boy of twelve years making my acquaintance with elementary mathematics, I was thrilled in seeing that it was possible to find out truth by reasoning alone, without the help of any outside experience...I became more and more convinced that even nature could be understood as a relatively simple mathematical structure. Albert Einstein, 1935, 12

Reasoning and Science

ANY BOOK OR OTHER METHOD of communication, which has the goal of discovering truth, should do the following things: rationally examine all evidence pointing toward or away from that perceived truth, determine the relevance of the evidence, and use those conclusions to define or reject the truth that is sought. This is called *deductive reasoning*.

The other approach to define a truth is to presume that truth and then gather evidence that supports or rejects that truth. When all evidence is interpreted, that preconceived truth will stand or be rejected. This is called *inductive reasoning*. Science has primarily developed using deductive reasoning since the purpose of science is typically not to prove a truth thought by others to exist but to establish a new truth, never before accepted or recognized.

Scientists have, over the years of practice, accepted the *scientific method* to determine *laws of science*. That method states that the evidence used to establish a law of science must be observed, documented, and repeatable by others. Any conclusion that cannot meet these requirements is relegated to the level of a *theory*, until it is proven by the three tests. The category of theory is where both the theory of Creation and the theory of evolution lie. A believer in the reality of the supernatural can argue that God observed Creation and He documented it, but it can't be repeated. Evolution was not observed or documented, and even though billions of dollars have been spent trying to repeat it, there has been no success.

There is more information available today than in any time in history. Do you want to know the truth, or are you satisfied with your own thoughts and those of your friends?

The Human Condition

We, as humans, find ourselves on this planet earth—initially existing as newborns—through no effort or intellect of our own. At the point in time of conception, we become human when, prior to that, we were not. That state of humanity carries with it a certain responsibility to use our minds and our brains to survive. At around the age of twenty-five, our brains have developed to the point that they are as capable of reasoning as they ever will be.

Our brains can be limited by reduced input. If a person has none of the five senses—sight, hearing, touch, taste, or smell—that person's brain would have no external input; therefore it would have no memories or thoughts. Thoughts require an input of experience. With no natural stimuli, there can be no thought, no reasoning, and no conclusions. Without stimuli a person would be mentally equivalent to a vegetable, unable to function. Einstein said, "The individual, if left alone from birth, would remain primitive and beastlike in his thoughts and feelings...The individual is what he is…by virtue [of being] a member of a great human community that directs his material and spiritual existence from cradle to grave."[1]

Some of our senses are more developed than others, and we are limited by this development, but we are still dependent on outside influences for our reasoning. How would our brains recognize a stimulus unless it had an external source? We can argue that our natural body can produce stimuli, but even that is external to our brains.

So we learn from others—nature and other humans—or we do not learn and do not think.

In 1952 Albert Einstein said, "What a person thinks on his own, without being stimulated by the thoughts and experiences of other people, is even in the best case rather paltry and monotonous."[2]

The Human Response

The ability we possess to think and reason through the input we receive from our senses, allows us uniquely to understand and respond. Because of an understanding of time—that events are unrepeatable when completed and unpredictable before completion—humans have a natural tendency to be curious about the future. We recognize death as the inevitable end of experience and accept that it may be internally within our control or externally out of our control.

During life most humans are social animals within or without their blood relationships. If we are not completely self-centered, we have an interest in the future of our family and our friends. That interest, as well as a study of history, should provide input to a better understanding of and reaction to the flow of life from past to present to future.

The Human Limitations

True science is limited to observation, control, and perhaps manipulation of nature. We cannot observe something that occurred before our birth, so all such occurrences must be repeated through the scientific method, ignored, or considered theory. This includes how humans—and prior to that, animals, vegetation, and inorganics—were originally formed. These questions remain theory, not science.

We can understand that all nature consists of inorganics, non-living organics, living organics, vegetative organics, animal organics, and human organics. We can experiment and theoretically understand and possibly even duplicate or control some of these components of nature.

We, as humans, take pride in our scientific advancement, especially as it relates to past levels of achievement. But is our discovery of scientific laws increasing? Research will indicate that the majority of scientific laws were discovered in the distant past and that new laws are being discovered with an increasing lapse of time in between. Have we answered the most elemental questions of nature?

- How were we created?
- How can we prevent death?
- What is mental illness, and how is it prevented?
- How do we reach peace in the world?
- What is the source of morality?
- Is there life in outer space?

All of these questions have one thing in common; they cannot be answered using the scientific method.

The Question Remains

There is a larger question that falls beyond science but can potentially answer all of these questions about life, death, and the future: *Is there a supernatural or spiritual reality in addition to the natural reality?*

Albert Einstein understood this question: "Mere unbelief in a personal God is no philosophy at all, and then there are the fanatical atheists whose intolerance is the same as the religious fanatics, and it springs from the same source...They are creatures who can't hear the music of the spheres."[3]

---

1 Alice Calaprice, *The New Quotable Einstein*, (Princeton, NJ: Princeton University Press, 2005) 201.
2 Ibid., 206.
3 Ibid., 204.

CHAPTER 3

The Problem of Existence

I assert that the cosmic religious experience is the strongest and the noblest driving force behind scientific research. Albert Einstein, 1930, 199

ONLY AN INTELLIGENT SOURCE—EVEN more, only a Creator—could negate natural evolutionary theory to allow the highest product (man) to not exist forever, as do the lower products.

Why would an all-powerful Creator allow His ultimate creation to be limited by death? Initially, He did not. He created a "good" world and universe and a "very good" human being—who had DNA but no capacity for death. (See Genesis 1:31, 2:17, 3:19, Romans 5:12, 15–17.)

That first human had the weakness of wanting to thoroughly understand his Creator—as have all humans since. Indeed he wanted to replace his Creator with himself. If we hold the mind-set that we truly have to understand everything that God has done, then when we—or some other human—cannot understand something, our stubbornness forces us to believe that *something* does not exist. At that point we want to be God. That selfish desire is impossible to realize since, by definition, God is the only entity that has existed forever, and He is the only explanation of where the universe came from. The only just penalty that a just God could have for His Creation wanting to take His place is death, in order to limit the sovereignty of humans. Because of death we could not be omniscient, omnipotent, or omnipresent like God. Along with that Fall of man, God also justly cursed all other living organic matter, vegetation, and animals, since these things provided man's sustenance.

In natural life the opposite of death is health, or life. Health is the balance between internal physical life and external nature, and everything outside of our bodies works toward our death. Organisms that allow us to live destroy us after death.

The only solution then to death—the problem of existence—was for God to personally enter our universe as a living, organic being in the form of Jesus Christ: fully human and fully God, incarnated—as was the whole universe—from nothing but God. As God He communicates to us, His Creation, His plan to return to us the opportunity of the original Creation: to exist forever.

This huge question of our acceptance of the supernatural must be answered if we are to understand the possibilities for the future of species—including how the natural and the supernatural relate. The overwhelming majority of the population has some belief in the supernatural. It may be New Age, reincarnation, mental telepathy, ghosts, Hinduism, Buddhism, Islam, Judaism, or Christianity, but it is based on spirituality as reality. The ability to recognize that reality is not limited to natural occurrences, and this is the key to understanding our relationship to our past, present, and future.

Many of us base our beliefs solely on the findings of science, as did Darwin. Natural science is limited to a study of the natural—those things in our universe that we can sense by sight, hearing, smell, taste, and physical feeling—and is incapable of analyzing the supernatural or spiritual. If there is only science, and no supernatural, there is no God. If science is our god, the accumulation of human knowledge is our truth and our bible, and that changes every day.

When we exclusively—through our efforts and intellect—attempt to discount or to explain the supernatural, we will become frustrated because the natural mind cannot completely understand the supernatural.

CHAPTER 4
Natural Reality

§

My scientific work is motivated by an irresistible longing to understand the secrets of nature and by no other feelings. My love for justice and the striving to contribute toward the improvement of human conditions are quite independent from my scientific interests. Albert Einstein, 1949, 14

ALL NATURAL THINGS ARE ORGANIC or inorganic chemically, and they are the basis, subject, and limitation of natural science. To discover more of natural reality, we must use our senses—and the senses of others—to observe, learn, and understand. There is a potential for completely grasping the wonders of nature including the past and present of human existence. If God created nature, we could never duplicate His intricate Creation, but there is still a potential for replacing parts of nature—including human parts—with synthetic parts. The better we understand God's Creation, the more efficient our efforts in this endeavor will become.

In this natural world, things exist in two ways: some seemingly permanent and others temporary, with a beginning and an end. One of the never disproven laws of science is that matter can be changed, but it can neither be created nor destroyed. Einstein proved that energy and mass are interchangeable through the theory of special relativity, $E=mc^2$. As long as *c*—the speed of light—is constant, there is a balance in the universe of mass plus energy. If that balance has ever or will ever be broken, the speed of light must change accordingly.

Since we see by applying the laws of science that matter can never be created, existence cannot have been naturally created, and it can't be naturally destroyed. Within inorganic nature, matter can be changed by chemical reactions. Within organic nature, the change of matter is caused by the separation or combination of carbon, oxygen, hydrogen, and inorganics. Therefore fundamental scientific law tells us that matter can be changed, but neither created nor destroyed.

The Natural Permanence of Nonliving Matter

Now, having said all of this, natural things exist as organics or inorganics. **Nonliving organics may have an expectancy of existence in their current form, but if they are broken down into a simpler form—or changed through heat and/or pressure—they may exist forever.** Many nonliving organics are derived from living organics. For instance, plants under pressure can form peat, which under heat and pressure can form coal, which under heat and pressure can form graphite and possibly diamonds, which can all—theoretically—last forever. Likewise, nonliving organics break down naturally through oxidation (fire or bacterial decomposition) into inorganics, the natural and permanent end to all existence. As per Einstein, mass may be converted to energy through unusual circumstances, but that mass or energy exists forever, given a constant speed of light.

Once the DNA has decomposed in a living organism through death, the remaining organics can combine with inorganics to form soil, sand, and rocks that theoretically exist forever.

In fact, as far as natural science is concerned, the molten and nonmolten rock core of our planet—and of all solid matter in the universe—is theoretically permanent.

As gases, the elements oxygen, nitrogen, hydrogen, and others have existed forever. They can't be destroyed, only changed.

As liquids, the water cycle has existed forever. There is a mass balance of water in our atmosphere, and all water has always existed in one of its three forms. Even before Noah's flood, water existed in vapor form as explained in Chapter 12.

Organics can be formed from carbon and hydrogen inorganics into hydrocarbons such as methane (CH^4); more complex organics formed from combinations of carbon and hydrogen, such as benzene, ethyl benzene, toluene, and xylene; even more complex organics formed from combinations of carbon, hydrogen, and oxygen (carbohydrates such as alcohols, ethers, amines, and pesticides); and combinations of hydrocarbons and inorganics, such as insecticides—like nicotine and DDT—and steroids such as cholesterol and testosterone.

In inorganic chemistry, inorganics can combine with hydrogen to form acids and ammonia, with hydroxide (OH) to form bases, and with each other to form salts—all of which can theoretically last forever.

So inorganics can be changed, but in their most elemental form, they exist forever. There is no death in relation to inorganics.

The Natural Death of Living Matter

Simple organics combined with things like acids, bases, and salts can theoretically form organic acids like amino acids, proteins, and nucleic acids such as DNA (deoxyribonucleic acid), the building block of life.

The basic difference between living organisms and nonliving organics is that living organisms contain this hereditary material called DNA, which stores information as a code made up of adenine, guanine, cytosine, and thymine. This code is ordered into about three billion bases (the rungs of the ladder), which are paired up with each other and attached to a sugar molecule and a phosphate molecule (the uprights of the ladder) to form the familiar double-helix spiral shape. The order or sequence of these bases determines the information available for building and maintaining an organism. This code programs the living organism to be a plant or an animal—and determines which type it is to be, including its unique characteristics within that type.

Science has spent billions of dollars trying to create life from the basic elements and has so far failed—and forever will—because DNA is so complex and includes preprogrammed directions to form life, which appear to be supernatural. Science can only create life from life that contains DNA, in the form of processes like cloning and grown body parts. Nature, not having intelligence, has no ability or capacity to program anything with intelligence.

When inorganic gases, liquids, and solids—and even some nonliving organics—exist forever, why do living organics alone in the universe have a life span? They don't exist forever. Is it because their DNA is faulty? What caused this dichotomy in nature? Why, through evolution, didn't inorganics evolve into nonliving organics, which in turn would evolve into living organics, which would be improved in their permanency? Instead, the higher levels of evolution have the greatest weakness; they die.

So, theoretically, living organisms should have evolved into permanence, not death. Therefore, there is no rational explanation for death through evolutionary theory. Death must have come from a supernatural source, outside of the universe and outside of our five senses. Death came from God as a curse for our demanding to take His place.

CHAPTER 5

Do We Accept a Supernatural Reality?

Try and penetrate with our limited means the secrets of nature and you will find that, behind all the discernible catenations, there remains something subtle, intangible, and inexplicable. Veneration for this force beyond anything that we can comprehend is my religion. To that extent I am, in point of fact, religious. Albert Einstein, 1927, 195

IN ORDER TO UNDERSTAND THE origin, the present, and the future of species, we must define reality. Webster says reality is "the quality or state of being real, of existing." Does the supernatural exist? Again, Webster says, "exist" means "to have reality." So even the definers of words end in cyclical reasoning.

Existence consists of all natural things that can be realized by one of our senses. Reality, but not existence, can also consist of things unrealized through our five senses. For example natural science can never prove or disprove supernatural reality, but that reality is the only explanation for much that we question or believe. Supernatural reality can only be discerned by our minds and is beyond the capability of science. How did the universe begin? How does prophecy work or mental telepathy? Are there a heaven and a hell? Is there such a thing as spirits, ghosts, evil, or good? Why do all civilizations independently define morality so similarly? Why does over 90 percent of the world's population believe in a supernatural God?

In order to discern the future of species, we must determine whether there is reality beyond the natural. If so, this supernatural reality must logically control the natural reality, or our natural brains would understand it. So either the supernatural is true and we don't understand it, or it is untrue and an imaginary delusion.

To understand natural reality, we must think deductively, since we can't know the whole natural truth that God created, nor does anyone. But to understand spiritual truths, we must think inductively, realizing the truth from our study of and belief in the Bible, and peeling back more and more layers of that truth using the infinate power of our indwelling Holy Spirit.

Our limitation in the understanding of spiritual reality is the fact that reasoning is a natural ability. **Since the spiritual realm overrules the natural realm, the spiritual relationship with the Ruler of the supernatural—God—is our only connection with that realm**. And the connection is unilateral—from God to us—since the supernatural is the more powerful and, therefore, controlling realm. All we can do is to accept that relationship, to answer the knock, and to submit to the control. That seems easy to say, but it is so hard to do—to let go of our control and let ourselves be under the control of an external spiritual force we can't see or completely understand. It seems so un-American, so weak, and so pathetic. But if we accept the necessarily submissive relationship between the ruled and the ultimate Ruler—and if we realize that the Ruler is just, fair, and desires good for us—we will gladly let go and submit through the belief, faith, and new birth that the Ruler has granted us.

We understand our limitations, and the limitations of mankind. The revelation of the acceptance of the supernatural is that it has no limit. With God, anything is possible, supernaturally and naturally. Miracles, past, present and future, are just a demonstration of God's power and grace, and should be a reason for praise and not a source of confusion or doubt.

Throughout the history of mankind, supernatural and natural reality have interrelated every day, as Satan has attempted to draw us away from God and God has continued to prevail. (See 1 Peter 5:8–9: "Be sober-minded; be watchful. Your adversary the devil prowls around like a roaring lion, seeking someone to devour. Resist him, firm in your faith.") Indeed, every miracle in the Bible, and those continuing even today, demonstrates the power of the supernatural over the natural. **But a few times in history, the supernatural has intervened in a way that has changed the natural permanently: the Creation itself; the writing and preservation of the Old Testament; Jesus's birth, which established the dating system of the world; Jesus's death and resurrection, which allowed us to communicate with a holy God and live with Him forever; and the writing and preservation of the New Testament.**

With acceptance of the supernatural reality comes the assurance that God will not end our reality with death. He has provided a permanent existence with Himself in heaven or in hell, depending on whether we have answered the knock and have given ourselves up in submission to our true Father. John 8:51 says, "Truly, truly, I say to you, if anyone keeps My word, he will never see death." And Romans 6:23 tell us "for the wages of sin is death, but the free gift of God is eternal life in Christ Jesus our Lord." Many more verses teach this critical truth, but one important aspect in understanding the issue is Satan's part. Satan, the author of lies, lied to Eve and promised that she would not die and that she would be like God if she followed his directions. (See Genesis 3:4–5.)

Hebrews 2:14 says, "Since therefore the children share in the flesh and blood, He Himself likewise partook of the same things, that through death He might destroy the one who has the power of death, that is, the devil." **So Satan has the power of death; he changed a created world with no death to a fallen world with death. He continues his destruction today as temptation, lies, and evil in his form as a fallen angel, prowling "around like a roaring lion, seeking someone to devour" (1 Peter**

5:8). But Jesus has defeated death, and His sacrifice has redeemed those who have accepted Him ("our Savior Christ Jesus, Who abolished death and brought life and immortality to light through the gospel" (2 Timothy 1:10)). So the supernatural reality is permanent and settled forever!

CHAPTER 6
Beliefs

Science without religion is lame, religion without science is blind. Albert Einstein, 1940, 203

ATHEISM

IF OUR PRESUPPOSITION OR BIAS is that there is no God, then we must rely on science and the accumulated knowledge of mankind to explain the origin, present, and future of the universe, and we will discuss these claims in this chapter. Atheists (those who believe there is no God) hold to the belief system and faith that time had no beginning, and original matter and energy always existed. Eventually, through chance, that matter and energy got together to start things off. This belief system substitutes the belief that basic matter has always existed for the scientific law that says that matter cannot be created; but it has the advantage of completely eliminating God from the question and, therefore, doing away with the difficulty of having to determine His involvement in the universe. In this view the mission statement—or document of belief—is the accumulated writings of scientists and philosophers since the beginning of Homo sapiens, as well as the hope, and even the faith, that humans will develop the knowledge to preserve the species in the future.

Atheism is not the lack of a religion; it is a religion itself. It requires a deep faith in the possibility that matter, and therefore time, could have existed forever with no beginning, and that random chance allowed the spontaneous generation through a convergence of inorganic matter into organic matter, DNA, living organisms, and later, the most complex structure ever made: humans. Atheism requires the faith that the laws of science are incorrect, and matter is getting better and more organized, instead of deteriorating. It requires a faith as strong as the likelihood of the Bible being cut into one letter pieces, dropped from an airplane, and landing in the form of the original Bible.

You can't definitely prove a negative—that there is no God. Therefore, atheists must put their faith in something or nothing. If nothing, they have no beliefs, and, therefore, no minds. So without God, they must invent a god, and it is typically nature or mankind: the faith that nature is benevolent and improving and that humans will acquire the unselfish wisdom to develop a self-sustaining civilization with permanent peace. Or, if they believe in science, they must accept the ultimate destruction of nature and mankind because of the law of entropy. In short, they lack the ability to cognitively think through history and realize that random chance will not allow evolution instead of devolution. Theologian R. C. Sproul said, "When scientists attribute instrumental power to chance, they have left the domain of physics and resorted to magic. Chance is their magic wand to make not only rabbits but entire universes appear out of nothing."[1]

I'll have to side with Einstein on atheism; an atheist must either be unable to reason or have a deep faith that "something" or "nothing" has caused matter to exist forever, with no beginning of time; or he must believe that, contrary to science, matter has emerged at the beginning of time from nothing.

Gerald L. Schroder, a prominent physicist said, "But before the universe, time did not exist. On the fact of time's nonexistence prior to the creation, theology and science are in complete agreement. So the beginning of the universe cannot be the effect of a cause. The universe must simply be."[2] Virtually all recent theological and scientific literature concedes that the universe had a beginning, and we should pronounce that Aristotle's idea of an eternal universe is dead!

Alvin Plantinga, who *Time* magazine called "the world's most important living Christian philosopher," describes philosophical naturalism (atheism) as "the view that there is no such person as God (no all-powerful, all knowing, and wholly good person who has created the world and has created human beings in his image), nor anything at all like God. The naturalist—the contemporary naturalist, at any rate—typically adds a high view of science, seeing it as the only possible source of our salvation."[3]

Theistic Evolution

Many believers in scientific law—who do not call themselves atheists, in order to eliminate the awkward necessity of ignoring those laws—accept that a supernatural God existed forever and, at some time in the distant past, created something from nothing that was the natural basis for matter, and allowed or caused energy and time to provide opportunity for different types of matter to combine to form more complex matter, which eventually would become inorganics, organics, living organics, plants, animals, and finally humans. This is called theistic evolution. This belief has the advantage of eliminating a God Who is involved with His Creation on a continuing basis, and as in the belief of atheists, has the hope that humans will develop the knowledge necessary to preserve the universe into the future.

In order to explain the continuation of the supernatural, some of these believers in a limited God—who started theistic evolution—accept that at the time when animals had evolved sufficiently, God placed a soul into the beast, and the animal became human. This view is forced to consider that the soul is a spiritual thing and brings the supernatural into the theory—in both the initial creation of the basis for matter and, later, in the importation of the soul. But God is then limited to certain actions. This is an advantage to these believers who prefer to have complete control, along with their peers, of the future of the universe—without dependence on an external force—while having the comfort of something out there that is "bigger than you or me." This is perhaps the simplest and easiest of the views of reality because it requires very little faith, only hope. It also allows for a multitude of different religions that believe in works of righteousness, rather than an active, controlling God. In that way it seems like a very tolerant and benevolent faith. **The major problem is that if these theistic evolutionists call themselves Christian, they must abandon** the words of the Founder of their religion and substitute the ever-evolving theory of evolution as their belief document.

Intelligent Design

The third popular view is that an intelligence created the universe supernaturally—over an unknown period of time but eventually all in place and operable, similar to the present—but that the intelligence has not and will not interfere with his creation, since he had the wisdom and power to create a universe that would evolve and be self-sustaining on its own. This view accepts that humans have the responsibility, through their works, of preserving the universe. **It has the advantage, as does the previous theistic evolution view, of allowing mankind to have control over its fate. It also shares the advantage of being rather simple to accept, without the difficulties of wrestling with the rules and directions of the God of the scriptures of the Holy Bible.** It also admits, as will any rational thinker, that spontaneous generation of matter is impossible. But it has the distinct disadvantage of refuting evolutionary teaching as accepted by many specialized scientists, and more importantly, does not conform to the teachings of most school systems in the world today. Consequently, these believers are not allowed to teach their belief system in public today.

Like theistic evolutionists, many intelligent-design believers may call themselves Christian, but again, they have lost their belief documents. In this case they have replaced the Bible with nothing but faith in their own theory and the comfort of compromise.

Judaism

Judaism is the oldest religion of the Western world, and the first to teach monotheism. The religion believes that God inspired the writings of the Hebrew Bible, what Christians call the Old Testament, and that Jewish priests were inspired to write the Talmud, a series of books of Jewish civil and religious laws and ethical lore derived from early oral laws.

Each Jewish congregation chooses its own rabbi but belongs to no international body with authority over religious practice. Today, the resultant belief differences are expressed through three major religious groups: Orthodox, Conservative, and Reformed. Orthodox Judaism believes that every word of the Pentateuch—the first five books of the Old Testament—and its interpretations in the Oral Law came from God on Mount Sinai. Conservative Judaism recognizes the authority of Jewish law but believes that the concept of revelation is subject to many interpretations. Reformed Judaism believes that each generation has the right to accept, reject, or modify the traditions it has received.

Faith in one God forms the basis of Judaism. Those who follow Judaism believe that God created man in His own image. Orthodox Jews believe that a personal Messiah, a descendent of the house of David, will come to redeem mankind on earth. Many Conservative and Reformed Jews believe that a Messianic Kingdom of Justice, a period of freedom and peace, will come with God's help and the efforts of men.[4]

CHRISTIANITY

The last view discussed in this book is that of Christianity. **There are many divergent views within Christianity, but the view that differentiates Christianity from cults and other beliefs is that Christianity is based on the teachings of its founder, Jesus Christ, and His inspiration found in the writings in the Old and New Testaments of the Holy Bible, called "the scriptures" by many Christians.** All believers who call themselves Christians accept the Bible as the founding document of their belief. Individual churches and individuals who call themselves Christians have taken various liberties with the translations and interpretations of the scriptures, in order to conform to specific beliefs, to become more relevant to society today, or to appear more acceptable—either to individuals, members, or society.

One of the most convenient and popular methods of accomplishing these liberties is to categorize certain passages of scripture as myths, rather than actual events. One of the most common divergences of opinion within the Christian church is the interpretation of Genesis 1–3 (Creation) and 6–9 (the Flood). The English Standard Version of the Bible, a relatively new and conservative version, summarizes the interpretations of the first passage in its "Introduction to Genesis, Genesis and Science," as follows:

> Faithful interpreters have offered arguments for taking the creation week of Genesis 1 as a regular week with ordinary days (the "calendar day" reading); or as a sequence of geological ages (the "day-age" reading); or as God's "workdays," analogous to a human workweek (the "analogical days" view); or as a literary devise to portray the Creation week as if it were a workweek, but with concern for temporal sequence (the "literary framework" view). Some have suggested that Genesis 1:2, "the earth was without form and void," describes a condition that resulted from Satan's primeval rebellion, which preceded the creation week (the "gap theory"). There have been other readings as well, but these five are the most common.[5]

A believer in God can certainly believe in theistic evolution, intelligent design, day age, or the literary framework, but a person who claims to believe God's Word cannot hold to these beliefs with theological or scientific integrity. For instance, the Presbyterian Church in America appointed a Creation Study Committee due to concern about ordaining pastors with diverging beliefs of Creation. The Committee was *unable to come to unanimity over the nature and duration of the Creation days.* The Creation Study Committee's report defines the Framework Interpretation as follows: "exegesis indicates that the scheme of the Creation Week itself is a poetic figure and that the several pictures of Creation history are set within the six workday frames not chronologically but topically."[6]

The committee affirmed the orthodox view of Creation but urged the church to recognize honest differences.[7] The Framework Interpretation representatives to the committee based their entire argument on Genesis

2:5–7: "When no bush of the field was yet in the land and no small plant of the field had yet sprung up—for the Lord God had not caused it to rain on the land, and there was no man to work the ground, and a mist was going up from the land and was watering the whole face of the ground—then the Lord God formed the man). They claimed that these verses speak of a different order and time for Creation than does Genesis 1 (Ibid., 23). But even a cursory reading of these verses shows no attempt to number or order the days. No vegetation was present before the dry land appeared in Day 3, and man had not been created. Rain has nothing to do with Creation, but it is logical to a scientist that a mist or spring would rise up from newly risen dry land and provide the necessary moisture for plant survival. Man was not required to work the ground until he planted cultivated plants in Day 6 and afterward. Therefore these verses are not a contradiction but a confirmation that Genesis 1 and 2 are consistent. Chapter 2 is simply a commentary on chapter 1 and a bridge to the explanation of the Fall in chapter 3.

Matthew 5:18 says, "For truly, I say to you, until heaven and earth pass away, not an iota, nor a dot, will pass from the Law until all is accomplished." The Literary Framework view is another example of how theologians attempt to change scripture to conform to a warped view of science…and end up looking foolish.

---

1 R. C. Sproul, *Not a Chance, God, Science and the Revolt against Reason* (Grand Rapids, MI: Baker Books, 1999).
2 Gerald L. Schroeder, *The Science of God* (New York, NY: Broadway Books, 1998).
3 Alvin Plantinga, *Darwin, Mind and Meaning* (Notre Dame, IN: University of Notre Dame, 1996), 1.
4 Philip S. Bernstein, *The World Book Encyclopedia, Judaism*, (Chicago, IL Field Enterprises Educational Corporation, 1977).
5 Desmond Alexander, "Introduction to Genesis, Genesis and Science," in *English Standard Version Study Bible* (Wheaton, IL:Crossway Bibles, 2008) 43.
6 *Report of the Creation Study Committee* (St Louis, MO: PCA Historical Center, 2005) 23.
7 Ibid., 34.

CHAPTER 7
The Belief Documents

§

*No one can read the Gospels without feeling the actual
presence of Jesus. His personality pulsates in every word.
No myth is filled with such life. Albert Einstein, 196*

As described above, each of the two principle beliefs concerning the origin of the universe has its own belief documents: evolution with its accumulated writings and Creation with its Bible. In this chapter I have selected a few well-written books in order to present a sense of the range of arguments for evolution. Since evolution is a theory and not a science, there is no set of rules or laws to limit the extent of the theories. Consequently, the theory of evolution has become an ever-evolving fantasy of imagination and is changing daily.

CREATION

THE HOLY BIBLE
I have read many translations of the Bible, and in my earlier years, I tried seriously to find contradictions within or between translations that would allow me the freedom to pick and choose my favorites. That effort was unsuccessful, and I have no recommended translations to offer.

"Translations" have different purposes: some are intended to be literal, some are intended to update language, some are paraphrases, and some are commentaries. All quotes in this book are from the English Standard Version translation.

That, along with the King James Version, the New King James, the New American Standard, and others are intended to be as literal as the English language allows. Paraphrases attempt to make the Bible more understandable, and are valuable for this reason, but should not be used as a literal word-for-word translation for in-depth study, because that is not their intent.

After wrestling with the Bible and its translations, I have come to believe in the inerrancy of scripture for the following reasons:

- I believe in the supernatural—a realm without time—that has always existed.
- I believe that a supernatural God created natural existence.
- I believe that God, by definition, is perfectly good, all-powerful in the supernatural and natural realms, all knowledgeable and always present in both realms.
- I believe that God is the very definition of love, truth, justice, and grace, and with those characteristics, He has elected to correspond with His highest level of Creation, through the most advanced technology at the time: the written word.
- I believe that God, when He corresponded in the original manuscripts, made no mistakes. In other words, His communication was perfect.
- **I believe that God has preserved the Holy Scriptures over time, through their translations, so that none of His truth as originally communicated is changed or lost. I do not believe that a loving, merciful, all-present, and powerful God would allow a lack of communication with His Creation. Man's mistakes cannot overcome God's purposes.**
- I believe that, at the proper time, God sent Jesus supernaturally into His Creation with the purpose of communicating further

truth and becoming a perfect sacrifice to pay the price for the sins of His fallen Creation.
- **I believe that Jesus Christ is the only explanation for the return of our relationship with a holy God.**
- I believe that Jesus left Himself as the Holy Spirit to enable each one of His chosen children to accurately interpret the Bible, if needed, on his own.

Concerning the Bible as the inerrant belief document of the Christian faith, I offer the following additional comments, some of which are taken from *A Christian Environmentalist*:[1]

- Virtually all organizations have a charter, a mission statement, by-laws, or some sort of written documentation to describe the group's purpose. An organization that ignores or changes these standards becomes a different organization from the original. It is certainly reasonable, and in some cases best, to change founding documents when those documents provide the mechanism for amendment. A government can acquire a different purpose or better provide for its constituents; a company can improve or expand its service, products or profits; a religion can adapt to the times and attract more followers; but a Christian church—even though it may have a statement or constitution that is subservient to the Bible that can be modified—is on a slippery slope if it ignores or changes the Bible, even in the slightest way. If left unchecked, reinterpreting the Bible will ultimately cause the church to lose its identity as a Christian church. It has lost its founding document, which was not written by human founders but was written by the supernatural Founder. **His document, His Bible, allows no provision for amendment, as explained above. Therefore, a Christian church that allows men to interpret the Holy Scriptures, instead of the Holy Spirit, has become a non-Christian sect—with man as its head, in place of God.**
- The Bible must be understood in context (i.e., the Bible interprets the Bible). All of the popular so-called discrepancies in the Bible

are taken out of context. For instance, in the Old Testament, there are books of history such as the Pentateuch (Genesis, Exodus, Leviticus, Numbers, Deuteronomy) and then Joshua through Job. There are books of poetry and wise sayings—such as Psalms, Proverbs, Ecclesiastes, and Song of Solomon—and books of prophesy, such as Isaiah through Malachi. Each type of book has its own consistent purpose and style of communication.

- In the New Testament, there are books of history—such as the Gospels Matthew, Mark, Luke and John, and The Acts of the Apostles—letters, such as Romans through Jude, and the prophetic book of Revelation. Each of these types of literature has its own structure and purpose.
- Most supposed contradictions come from either Proverbs or the Gospels. Proverbs, in context, is a book of Solomon's wise and true sayings, which—as in life today—teach one action or response in one case and perhaps an opposite action or response in another case. Observers who witnessed events or researched them (Luke) wrote the Gospels and emphasized different and similar events.
- **By virtually all definitions, God is supernatural, supreme, the Creator, omniscient (has infinite knowledge), omnipresent (present everywhere at all times), omnipotent (has unlimited power), and omnibenevolent (has perfect goodness).**
- A perfect God logically must do everything perfectly, or He wouldn't be God. This includes communication with His creation. He has elected to communicate in the written and created forms—the written form being the most advanced technology of communication available at the time of the writings and the created form being the obvious example of His work. God appointed the Hebrew people to copy the manuscripts as originally authored ("Then what advantage has the Jew? Or what is the value of circumcision? Much in every way. To begin with, the Jews were entrusted with the oracles of God" Romans 3:1–2). By law these scribes transcribed these manuscripts perfectly, or the manuscripts

were destroyed. The success of this practice has been confirmed by comparing transcribed manuscripts discovered many centuries ago with those that were transcribed even earlier but not discovered until 1947 (the Dead Sea Scrolls).[2]

- Christians, and Jews accepting Jesus Christ as their Savior, are the new Israel and are now responsible for preserving God's Holy Word. Consider the following verses: "This is how one should regard us, as servants of Christ and stewards of the mysteries of God" (1 Corinthians 4:1). "Or is God the God of Jews only? Is He not the God of Gentiles also? Yes, of Gentiles also, since God is one—who will justify the circumcised by faith and the uncircumcised through faith" (Romans 3:29–30). "But it is not as though the Word of God has failed. For not all who are descended from Israel belong to Israel, and not all are children of Abraham because they are his offspring, but 'Through Isaac shall your offspring be named.' This means that it is not the children of the flesh who are the children of God, but the children of promise are counted as offspring" (Romans 9:6–8). (See also Hosea 2:23, Romans 9:24, 10:12, 11:25–27, 15:8–21, and Galatians 4:28.)

Therefore it is logical that a perfect and good God would communicate the truth of His desire to spend eternity with His creation in a perfect way, without error, and that through His omnipotence, He would assure that translations are faithful as He intended.

This is why I believe that the Bible, in its original documents, is inerrant and infallible and, in its literal translations, contains God's communicated truth without error.

Infinitely more important than my acceptance of the Bible as inerrant is what the Bible says about itself. Here are a few of God's words concerning His communication with us:

- "Everything that I command you, you shall be careful to do. You shall not add to it or take from it" (Deuteronomy 12:32).

- "For truly, I say to you, until heaven and earth pass away, not an iota, nor a dot, will pass from the Law until all is accomplished (Matthew 5:18).
- "For whatever was written in former days was written for our instruction, that through endurance and through the encouragement of the Scriptures we might have hope" (Romans 15:4).
- "Knowing this first of all, that no prophesy of Scripture comes from someone's own interpretation. For no prophesy was ever produced by the will of man, but men spoke from God as they were carried along by the Holy Spirit" (2 Peter 1:20–21).
- "[J]ust as our beloved brother Paul also wrote to you according to the wisdom given him, as he does in all his letters as he speaks in them of these matters. There are some things in them that are hard to understand, which the ignorant and unstable twist to their own destruction, **as they do the other Scriptures**" (2 Peter 3:15–16).
- "But we have renounced disgraceful, underhanded ways. We refuse to practice cunning or to tamper with God's Word" (2 Corinthians 4:2).
- "I warn everyone who hears the prophesy of this book: if anyone adds to them, God will add to him the plagues described in this book" (Revelation 22: 18).

NATURE

God has blessed us with two types of revelation: natural, what God has made, and special, what God has said. Both are true. Any contradiction results from interpreting one or both incorrectly. "For what can be known about God is plain to them, because God has shown it to them. For His invisible attributes, namely, His eternal power and divine nature, have been clearly perceived, ever since the Creation of the world, in the things that have been made. So they are without excuse" (Romans 1:19–20). Also see Job 12:7–16, 35:10–12, 37:1–24, Psalms 8:1–9, 19:1–6, Acts 14:17, 17:23–28, and Romans 10:16–18.

Evolution

Introduction
Writings promoting the theory of evolution began long before Darwin was born. In the sixth century BC, the Greek philosopher Anaximander wrote that the earth was condensed from water to mud, from which rose plants and animals and later, from the sea, humans. Anaxagoras, in the fifth century BC, proposed that a principle that he called *mind* brought order from empty chaos. The Frenchman Buffon and James Hutton developed the theory of uniformitarianism in the eighteenth century. During this same time period, Erasmus Darwin, Charles Darwin's grandfather from England, set out the principles that form the basis of more recent evolutionary theory. In the nineteenth century, Karl Marx wrote about *The Origin of Species*, "this is the book which contains the basis in natural history for our view."[3]

The Origin of Species, Charles Darwin[4]
As indicated by its title, the document is limited in scope to botanical and biological species. The book is probably best summarized in its last sentence, which reads, "There is grandeur in this view of life, with its several powers, having been originally breathed into a few forms or into one; and that, whilst this planet has gone cycling on in according to the fixed law of gravity, from so simple a beginning endless forms most beautiful and most wonderful have been, and are being, evolved."

All Darwin ended up accomplishing in this book was to document what he called *variation*, and today is called *microevolution*, which is obvious to almost anyone. This is the evolution within a kind—for instance from a wolf to a German shepherd to a poodle—or within various insect or bird species, either domestic or wild. **The evolution that we call *macroevolution*—which is said to occur between species—Darwin, nor anyone else, has ever documented.**

Since Darwin published his theory of evolution in 1859, there have been thousands of articles and books attempting to explain evolution further. The subject has been fraught with proponent disagreement and controversy, with no clear explanation or conclusion to date. The reason is that the causes and effects of evolution are all naturally based, and there has been no consistent scientific evidence to justify an explanation and conclusion or to transform a theory into a law. Even though there is no consensus, the book you are reading will quote from and credit many evolutionary texts in order to offer a sense of the progress toward evolutionists' goal of complete acceptance of a law of evolution.

GENESIS: THE SCIENTIFIC QUEST FOR LIFE'S ORIGIN, ROBERT HAZEN[5]

This book gallantly attempts to answer the question of how nonliving chemicals became alive through a system of *emergence*, by which "more complex systems arise from simpler systems, often in unpredictable fashion." The following quotes from the preface seem to outline the concept of the question and the theory: **"The Biblical account in the first chapter of Genesis, though rich in poetic metaphor, hardly puts the origin question to rest. Barring divine intervention, life must have emerged by a natural process—one fully consistent with the laws of chemistry and physics."** Again, as in the case of Darwin, Hazen is forthcoming about the limitations of his theory and leaves the door open to "divine intervention," an arena that he apparently feels unqualified to explore. Hazen goes on further to say, "Alternatively, the universe may be organized in such a way that life emerges as an inevitable consequence of chemistry, given an appropriate environment and sufficient time. Starting with water, organic molecules, and a suitably protected energy-rich environment, life may be very likely to emerge from nonlife on any hospitable planet or moon." Notice that Hazen starts with water and organic chemicals in a suitable environment. He does not argue for spontaneous generation.

THE FUTURE OF MANKIND, PIERRE TEILHARD[6]

Teilhard's theory of the future of man from inorganics to human civilization is written from a Christian perspective but using a theistic evolutionary approach. His Jesuit Order has rejected many of his views, and the Roman Catholic Church has censored some. Yet, many have extensively studied and carried on his works in the late twentieth and the twenty-first centuries.

In chapter 3, section 5, Teilhard says the following:

> Specifically our awareness of the world was extended to embrace the Infinitesimal and the Immense. Later, in temporal terms, there came the unveiling, behind us and ahead, of the abyss of past and future. Finally, to complete the structure we became aware of the fact that, within this indefinite extent of space-time, the position of each element was so intimately bound up with the genesis of the whole that it was impossible to alter it at random without rendering it "incoherent," or without having to readjust the distribution and history of the whole around it. To accommodate this expansion of our thought the restricted field of static juxtaposition was replaced by a field of evolutionary organization which was limitless in all directions (except forward, in the direction of its pole of convergence). It became necessary to transpose our physics, biology, and ethics, even our religion, into this new sphere, and this we are in the process of doing.

In chapter 6, section I, Teilhard goes on in this way:

> At the very beginning, so the astronomers tell us—that is to say, billions of years ago—there was in place of the present world a diffused atmosphere, billions of times less dense than air, spreading in all directions over billions of miles. This "primordial chaos," as

Jeans calls it, must have seemed homogeneous, but inasmuch as it was subject to the force of gravity, it was excessively unstable.

In section I.2 of chapter 6, Teilhard says this:

> The atom, the molecule, the cell, and the living being are real units because they are both formed and centrated, whereas a drop of water, a heap of sand, the Earth, the Sun, the stars in general, whatever the multiplicity or elaborateness of their structure, seem to possess no organization, no "centricity." However imposing their extent they are false units, aggregates arranged more or less in order of density…Despite their vastness and splendor the stars cannot carry the evolution of matter much beyond the atomic series: it is only on the very humble planets, on them alone, that the mysterious ascent of the world into the sphere of high complexity has a chance to take place.

In Section II he continues:

> If the essential function and dignity of the Earth consist in its being one of the rare laboratories where, in time and space, the synthesis of ever larger molecules is proceeding; and if, as our table of complexity shows, living organisms, far from originating in germs fallen upon Earth from the celestial spaces, are simply the highest composites to spring from planetary geochemism…then the discovery of Man's absolute place in the Universe becomes simply a matter of deciding what position we who constitute Mankind occupy in the evolving range of super-molecules."

In section III of chapter 6, Teilhard goes on to imagine a "planetary totalization of human consciousness":

First the vitalization of matter, associated with the grouping of molecules; then the hominization of Life, associated with a super-grouping of cells; and finally the planetization of Mankind, associated with a closed grouping of people: Mankind, born on this planet and spread over its entire surface, coming gradually to form around its earthly matrix a single, major organic unity, enclosed upon itself; a single hypercomplex, hypercentrated, hyperconscious arch molecule, coextensive with the heavenly body on which it was born.

Teilhard goes on further to describe this **"superorganism which, woven of the threads of individual men" and including the "tightening network of economic and psychic bonds in which we live, and from which we suffer," is the only theory "which affords a coherent prospect wherein, in the remote future, the deepest and most powerful currents of human consciousness may converge and culminate: intelligence and action, learning and religion."**

So, Teilhard is imagining a spiritual escape through the excess of consciousness, rather than a "period of euphoria and abundance…some form of threadbare millennium" (chapter 22). Some commentators consider Teilhard's "planetization of Mankind" theory a prediction of the ultimate evolution of the Internet.

GOD AND THE NEW PHYSICS, PAUL DAVIES[7]

Paul Davies does an excellent job in this book explaining many of the more recent theories of Creation from an evolutionary scientist's perspective. He begins in chapter 1 saying, "Science and religion represent two great systems of human thought. For the majority of people on our planet, religion is the predominant influence over the conduct of their affairs. When science impinges on their lives, it does so not at the intellectual level, but practically, through technology."

Davies goes on to speak of the big bang theory and how some Christians use it to support Creation. He says, **"If we accept that space and time really did erupt out of nothing in the big bang, then clearly there was a creation and the universe has a finite age."** But then he states, **"Though present scientific opinion lends strong support to the creation theory, it is important to realize that there is no logical reason why the universe cannot be infinitely old."** Davies says that scientific advances do not explain "[T]he creation of matter out of nothing, but the conversion of preexisting energy into material form" as per Einstein's theories. In order to explain this he writes two pages in chapter 3 with phrases like "seems legitimate," "inherently unpredictable," "probability," "finite chance," "loose causation," and "problems of self-consistency." This is hardly science speaking.

Davies's explanation of the cosmological argument is "the galaxies form from swirling nebulae, the nebulae form from primeval hydrogen gas, the hydrogen forms from the protons created in the first brief bang, the protons were created out of spacewarps."

Davies explains in chapter 8, "The Quantum Factor," the theories of "daughter universes," as per Einstein's theory of general relativity, and "myriads of parallel universes," as per Hugh Everett, but arrives at no conclusions, as is the curse of theoretical physics.

---

1 E. Roberts Alley, *A Christian Environmentalist* (USA: Xulon Press, 2013).
2 Randall Price, *Secrets of the Dead Sea Scrolls* (San Marcos, TX: World of the Bible Ministries, Inc., 1996).
3 Michael Pitman, *Adam and Evolution, A Scientific Critique of Neo-Darwinism* (Baker Book House, 1974), 24.
4 Charles Darwin, "Recapitulation and Conclusion," in *The Origin of Species*, 1859 (New York, NY: Bantam Books, 1999) 400.
5 Robert Hazen, *Genesis: The Scientific Quest for Life's Origins* (Washington, DC: The National Academies Press, 2005).
6 Pierre Teilhard de Chardin, *The Future of Mankind* (New York, NY: Harper & Row, 1959).
7 Paul Davies, *God and the New Physics* (New York, NY: Simon & Schuster, 1983).

Part 2
The Origin through Creation

CHAPTER 8

Introduction

*I want to know how God created the world. I am not
interested in this or that phenomenon, in the spectrum
of this or that element, I want to know his thoughts.
The rest are details. Albert Einstein, 1920, 194*

THE ORIGIN OF THE UNIVERSE—nor any of the major parts thereof, such as inorganics, organics, vegetation, animals, or humans—can possibly be explained or discovered through science, since science is limited to the study of matter, energy, and time that can be observed, documented, and repeated. As explained above, the original creation of these parts can never meet the requirements of science and will forever remain theories.

A theory, even a scientific one, does not necessarily have any rules. An honest scientist will desire to have his theories become law, or his work is futile as a scientist and unnecessary to civilization—other than for science-fiction entertainment. But outside of science, our reasoning effort and ability can open doors of understanding in the supernatural realm, if we subject our thought process to the guidance of the Holy Spirit. Francis Schaeffer says, "The beginning of the Christian view of nature is that God was there before the beginning and God created everything out of nothing. From this, we must understand that creation is not an extension of the essence of God. Created things have an existence in themselves. They are really there."[1]

Once we leave science, and its rules and laws, we certainly have the right to entertain others and ourselves with our imagination. One such diversion is religion. Religion is defined as "the service and worship of God or the supernatural."[2] Religion, to those who believe the Bible, is as old as mankind and is based on a belief in God. Since God is supernatural by nature, we can develop no rules to define or limit Him outside of the Bible, if we believe God exercised the power to control His communication with His Creation, as explained above.

Therefore any rational discussion of the characteristics or accomplishments of God must start and end with the Bible. In other wordsSo, this Part of the book, or any book, **there is no extra Biblical source of information about the supernatural. We can't scientifically experiment with the supernatural, as much as we would like to.** examining the spiritual reality, must concentrate on God's communication to us through His Word.

In this chapter, and in the rest of this book, pronouns describing God, Jesus or the Holy Spirit are capitalized, as in most literal translations of the Bible, in order to give more clarity to the text, even though this practice is not followed in the English Standard Version.

---

1 Francis A. Schaeffer, *Pollution and the Death of Man* (Wheaton, IL: Tyndale House Publishers, 1975),47
2 *Webster's Ninth New Collegiate Dictionary*, Frederick C. Mish, ed. (Springfield, Mass.: Merriam-Webster Inc.),1990.

CHAPTER 9

The Beginning of Supernatural Reality

§

I cannot prove scientifically that Truth must be conceived as a truth that is valid independent of humanity, but I firmly believe it...If there is a reality independent of man, there is also a truth relative to this reality...The problem begins with whether Truth is independent of our consciousness...For instance, if nobody is in this house, that table remains where it is. Albert Einstein, 1930, 197

THE BIBLE MAKES THE BEGINNING of supernatural reality very clear in the first verse of Genesis: "In the beginning, God created the heavens and the earth."

Outside of Genesis, both Old and New Testament passages make it clear that God created all of the heavens and the earth from nothing:

> "By the word of the Lord the heavens were made, and by the breath of His mouth all their host. He gathers the waters of the sea as a heap; He puts the deeps in storehouses. Let all the earth fear the Lord; let all the inhabitants of the world stand in awe of Him! For He spoke, and it came to be; He commanded, and it stood firm" (Psalms 33:6–9).

Here are additional verses to support this view:

- "Before the mountains were brought forth, or ever You had formed the earth and the world, from everlasting to everlasting You are God" (Psalms 90:2).
- "He answered, 'Have you not read that He Who created them from the beginning made them male and female'" (Matthew 19:4).
- "In the beginning was the Word, and the Word was with God, and the Word was God" (John 1:1).
- "All things were made through Him, and without Him was not any thing made that was made" (John 1:3).
- "He was in the world, and the world was made through Him, yet the world did not know Him" (John 1:10).
- "because You loved Me before the foundation of the world" (John 17:24).
- "a living God, Who made the heaven and the earth and the sea and all that is in them" (Acts 14:15b).
- "yet for us there is one God, the Father, from Whom are all things and for Whom we exist, and one Lord Jesus Christ, through Whom are all things and through Whom we exist" (1 Corinthians 8:6).
- "[T]he God in Whom he believed, Who gives life to the dead and calls into existence the things that do not exist" (Romans 4:17b).
- **"For by Him all things were created, in heaven and on earth, visible and invisible, whether thrones or dominions or rulers or authorities—all things were created through Him and for Him. And He is before all things, and in Him all things hold together" (Colossians 1:16-17).**
- "His Son, Whom He appointed the heir of all things, through Whom also He created the world" (Hebrews 1:2b).
- "[A]nd He upholds the universe by the word of His power" (Hebrews 1:3b).

- "By faith we understand that the universe was created by the word of God, so that what is seen was not made out of things that are visible" (Hebrews 11:3).
- "That Which was from the beginning" (I John 1:1a).
- "[F]or You created all things, and by Your will they existed and were created" (Revelation 4:11b).

These verses, and many others—including the direct words of Jesus—show that God's clear message to us in both Testaments is that He created the supernatural and the natural, and our efforts to prove otherwise will always be futile.

If a Christian attempts to ignore the story of the Creation or classify it as a myth or within a "literary framework" or subcategorizes parts of Genesis as nonhistorical and inaccurate in order to accommodate the latest theories of science he or she needs to consider carefully. This Christian is ignoring Jesus's statements: "For truly, I say to you, until heaven and earth pass away, not an iota, not a dot, will pass from the Law until all is accomplished" (Matthew 5:18) and when He said, "For if you believed Moses, you would believe Me; for he wrote of Me. But if you do not believe his writings, how will you believe My words?" (John 5:46–47). This Christian also risks breaking the ordinances of Moses (Deuteronomy 4:2, 12:32) and Jesus (Revelation 22:18–19).

There are obviously books of poetry in the Bible, but once we begin to interpret historical books of the Bible as poetry or fiction, rather than as truth, we grant ourselves and those we teach the right of interpreting the Bible for our convenience, rather than as an expression of God's character. If we base our belief in, and interpretation of the Bible on, something as weak and theoretical as a scientific theory, we make science and ourselves God. All truth is God's truth!

God placed Genesis as the first book of the Bible and chapter 1, verse 1 as the first verse. The first four words of this verse seem to contain one of the Bible's primary truths: *In the beginning, God.* If we can understand that God began reality, spiritual and natural, many of our questions are answered. Those four words introduce a series of deep philosophical and scientific truths that we need to love, to covet, and to pattern our lives around. We will examine those first truths as the six days of Creation.

CHAPTER 10

Day One of Creation, the Earth

*If God created the world, his primary concern
was certainly not to make its understanding
easy for us. Albert Einstein, 1954, 207*

THE FIRST SENTENCE OF THE first chapter of the first book of the Bible is Genesis 1:1: "In the beginning, God created the heavens and the earth." This verse tells us that in the beginning of time and natural existence, God created all natural matter—in space and on earth. The Hebrew word *genesis* means "origin" or "source."

The Hebrew word for God, *Elohim*, is plural, and the following word for created, *bara* is singular. In the Old Testament *bara* always has *Elohim* as its subject. So in the very first verse of the Bible, God makes the Trinity known; the *plural God* created the heavens and the earth as *one God*. The Trinity is eternally existent. All spirituality proceeds from the Trinity. Romans 1:20 says, "For His invisible attributes, namely His eternal power and divine nature, have been clearly perceived, ever since the creation of the world, in the things that have been made. So they are without excuse." Skeptics and unbelievers have no excuse for their lack of understanding, since God's power and nature are evident through the design, complexity, and uniqueness of what we can all easily observe.

Genesis 1:2 tells us that "the earth was without form and void, and darkness was over the face of the deep. And the Spirit of God was hovering over the face of the waters."

The word translated "without form" in this verse is *tohu* in Hebrew, meaning confusion and emptiness, symbolizing the state of an unregenerated soul—confused and empty. This same word is translated "confusion" in Isaiah 24:14 and 34:11. When Jeremiah quotes Genesis 1:2 in Jeremiah 4:23, he again uses *bohu* for "void" and *tohu* for "without form." There was no light, just as it is with us as unregenerated souls, without God; everything was confused and empty. But in this first day, **God created a light without the sun, just as He can do in us. God could have easily made His world perfect and complete initially, but instead He developed it sequentially to teach us about the method of His providence and grace and about His careful preparation for our dwelling place.** Again, the analogy is the development of our souls for our eternal presence with Him. God does not waste words or make them confusing and hard to understand.

2 Peter 3:5b says, "the earth was formed out of water and through water by the word of God" Job 26:7 says that God "stretches out the north over the void [*tohu*] and hangs the earth on nothing."

Psalms 104:5–6 says that God "set the earth on its foundations, so that it should never be moved" and that He "covered it with the deep." See also Amos 5:8.

Therefore, on day one, God created a dark, formless, and lifeless earth, made of inorganics in the form of a mineral core foundation, covered with water. The first sphere of nature required for life, the *hydrosphere*, was created on the first day—and would shortly provide the resource for sustenance for His final and ultimate Creation. The water was without form until the second day, when the waters were divided. Apparently the earth was not spinning or moving at that time, since there was no universe to cause it to spin or move. But over the face of the waters the first day, He infused the primitive natural with the supernatural Spirit of God. So the Holy Spirit was present as God to do God's will on the first day of

Creation, and He remains present today in His new temple, the bodies of the saints.

On the first day, God also created light and darkness, which He called day and night. (Genesis 1:3–5a says, "And God said, 'Let there be light,' and there was light. And God saw that the light was good. And God separated the light from the darkness. God called the light Day, and the darkness He called Night".) Already in this very first day, God gave us a spiritual light that we may forever see His good works and glory. As the Spirit gave light in day one, that same Spirit continues to move in our lives today, enlightening us to His truth and dispelling our natural darkness.

In verse 4 the light was called *good*, while the formless and dark void was not. Of this first day's creation, only light could support man; therefore, only light was "good." God also calls the Creation in days three, four, and five *good*, and day six He called His Creation *very good*. In 2 Corinthians 4:6 we read, "For God, Who said, 'Let light shine out of darkness,' has shone in our hearts to give the light of the knowledge of the glory of God in the face of Jesus Christ." The entire Old Testament is a description of the saving work of Jesus. This *light* is one of the earliest such references.

Get ready! We are starting to see that the Bible is a spiritual and supernatural book, and remember, the supernatural trumps the natural. It is more real, more lasting, and more important. The spiritually created light of Genesis 1:3–4 precedes and supersedes the natural sunlight of Genesis 1:14–18. Creation is just another supernatural miracle from God, no different from the many other Old and New Testament miracles we typically accept without question.

The sun was not created until the fourth day (verses 14–18). Apparently, the light of the first day in this perfected earth was the same light that Revelation describes in chapter 21, verse 23, as the light of the Lamb, Jesus: "And the city has no need of sun or moon to shine on it, for the glory of God gives it light, and its lamp is the Lamb." There was no need for the sun or the moon, for a superior spiritual light shone. **The power that made light out of darkness at Creation also disperses the darkness of sin in**

our hearts through the light of Christ at our spiritual Creation. John 1:9–10 says, "The true light, which enlightens everyone, was coming into the world. He was in the world, and the world was made through Him, yet the world did not know Him."

Since Jesus was present at Creation…
"In the beginning was the Word" (John 1:1a)
…and Jesus is designated as the Word."

And the Word was with God, and the Word was God. He was in the beginning with God. All things were made through Him, and without Him was not any thing made that was made. In Him was life, and the life was the light of men. The light shines in the darkness, and the darkness has not overcome it (John 1: 1b–5).

That which was from the beginning, which we have heard, which we have seen with our eyes, which we looked upon and have touched with our hands, concerning the Word of life—the life was made manifest, and we have seen it, and testify to it and proclaim to you the eternal life, which was with the Father and was made manifest to us—that which we have seen and heard we proclaim also to you, so that you too may have fellowship with us; and indeed our fellowship is with the Father and with His Son Jesus Christ (1 John 1: 1–3).

We can be assured that His Word—as communicated to us through the Holy Scriptures in both Testaments—is true and without error.
Genesis 1:8b continues, "And there was evening and there was morning, the second day." This is the first of six uses of this phrase "there was evening and there was morning." Genesis 1:8 describes the end of the first day's work. As part of the Fourth Commandment, Exodus 20: 11 says, "For in six days the Lord made heaven and earth, the sea, and all that is in them, and rested on the seventh day. Therefore the Lord blessed the Sabbath day and made it holy." So God selected a day of time for each step of His Creation and a week of time for the completion of His Creation and

the associated rest. Unless this timing was significant, there would have been no reason for mentioning it. **He could have just as easily completed Creation in a second or in a billion years. But He chose not to in order to teach us the lessons of timely work, rest, and worship.**

The spontaneous-generation theorists agree with God, that the universe began with inorganics, but unlike the Bible, they have no plausible explanation for the appearance of inorganic matter from nothing. Even Darwin could not make that unscientific leap of faith.

CHAPTER 11

Day Two of Creation, the Sky

§

The scientist is possessed by a sense of universal causation... His religious feeling takes the form of a rapturous amazement at the harmony of natural law, which reveals an intelligence of such superiority that, compared with it, all the systematic thinking and acting of human beings is an utterly insignificant reflection...It is beyond question closely akin to that which has possessed the religious geniuses of all ages. Albert Einstein, 1934, 201

ON DAY TWO—GENESIS 1:6–8—God created the sky ("heaven" or "firmament") and caused it to separate the waters underneath (the global ocean) and the waters above (the atmospheric water): "And God said, 'Let there be an expanse in the midst of the waters, and let it separate the waters from the waters'. And God made the expanse and separated the waters that were under the expanse from the waters that were above the expanse. And it was so. And God called the expanse Heaven."

The hovering Spirit, after creating light, created the second sphere of our existence, the *atmosphere*.

The firmament—*raqia* in Hebrew—is used consistently throughout the Old Testament and is translated also as "expanse," "canopy," or "heavens."

So far, God had spent two days creating inorganic matter in the form of water and minerals, which cannot chemically be created or destroyed. There was, as yet, no rain (Genesis 2:5) or organics, and unlike the next four days, God did not pronounce this lifeless day *good*. There were apparently no new elements or molecules created, but rather an ordering of the day-one Creation. God's purpose of Creation, humans, could still not be sustained.

Evolutionary theory, including Darwin's, avoids this biblical and necessary step of the origin. **God is the Creator of order, rather than the chaos of day one**. God continued to create more and more complex order in subsequent days. This is in contrast to Darwin, who started with simple—but created—organics and in contrast to other evolutionists who began with preexisting inorganics.

CHAPTER 12

Day Three of Creation, Vegetation

I have found no better expression than "religious" for confidence in the rational nature of reality, insofar as it is accessible to human reason. Whenever this feeling is absent, science degenerates into uninspired empiricism. Albert Einstein, 1951, 206

ON THE THIRD DAY OF Creation, described in Genesis 1:9–12, God separated the dry land from the seas and created the first organics: "And God said, 'Let the waters under the heavens be gathered together into one place, and let the dry land appear.' And it was so. God called the dry land Earth, and the waters that were gathered together He called Seas. And God saw that it was good."

The Spirit was still hovering over the created world, and in Day Three it caused dry land—the *lithosphere*—to appear out of the *hydrosphere*, giving us further organization and the last necessary sphere for our existence. God designed the *lithosphere* to support the *biosphere*, starting with vegetation and ending with humans. This miracle of dry land created out of chaos, is a metaphor for the miracle He performs today every time He raises a sinner out of the depths and chaos of his sin.

Psalms 104:6–7 speaks of God's rebuke that caused the waters to flee and the mountains to rise, to set boundaries for the waters: "You covered it with the deep as with a garment; the waters stood above the mountains. At Your rebuke they fled; at the sound of Your thunder they took to flight."

Genesis 1:11–13 says the following:

> And God said "Let the earth sprout vegetation, plants yielding seed, and fruit trees bearing fruit in which is their seed, each according to its kind, on the earth." And it was so. The earth brought forth vegetation, plants yielding seed according to their own kinds, and trees bearing fruit in which is their seed, each according to its kind. And God saw that it was good. And there was evening and there was morning, the third day.

These plants and fruit trees were created not as seeds, but as renewable plants of apparently sufficient age to yield seed and fruit with seeds. Did the trees have rings, indicating age, when they were created? Probably, since they were trees and not some prehistoric semblance of trees. The plants and the trees were described three times as being created *each according to its kind*. So God created the distinctiveness of DNA within a species or *kind* as soon as He created the first organics.

Other more accepted miracles, such as Jesus turning water into wine, various healings, and the feeding of the four thousand and the five thousand, also demonstrate creation with apparent age. Jesus created something with an apparent history through miracles just as amazing and inexplicable as the creation of water, air, land, vegetation, animals, and humans with an apparent age and history.

For the first time, God said that His natural Creation was good. The spiritual light described in verse 4 was called good, but it was supernatural and not natural. Even though Genesis 2:5 says that there was no rain at this time, there was a mist from the earth that watered the whole earth. (Genesis 2:5–6 says, "When no bush of the field was yet on the land and no small plant of the field had yet sprung up—for the Lord God had not caused it to rain on the land, and there was no man to work the ground, and a mist was going up from the land and was watering the whole face of the ground.")

This mist that rose from the ground prior to day three provided water for the plants formed in day three, but it also apparently provided a vapor canopy over the earth (the "waters above the expanse" from verse 7). Noah's Flood, as described in Genesis 6–8, rose to an elevation of approximately 16,876 feet above mean sea level.[1] Calculations have shown that the volume of water it would take to reach this level, if evaporated, would form a dense vapor canopy sufficient to diffuse solar radiation to the extent that animals and humans would live much longer, even to the ages listed in the Bible. It is of interest that the flood waters prevailed for 150 days (Genesis 7:24), abated over another 150 days (Genesis 8:3), and dried over seventy days (Genesis 8:14)—a total of approximately a year.

The ages of men listed in the Bible, from Adam to Noah, averaged almost nine hundred years. And the oldest human on record, Methuselah, lived for 969 years and died the year of the flood. (See Genesis 6:26–29, 7:6.) In Genesis 6:3, God said just before the flood, "My Spirit shall not abide in man forever, for he is flesh: his days shall be 120 years." Between Noah and Terah, Abraham's father, the ages upon death gradually decreased.

Another interesting conclusion is that dinosaurs became so large because of the longer lifespans that could be achieved due to thisvapor canopy protection, since it is a well-known fact that reptiles continue to grow their entire lives.[2]

There was no sun during day three; therefore, there was no photosynthesis to allow the plants to grow. Genesis 2:5 also addresses the importance of man in relation to the environment's vegetation, pointing out that there was no "man to work the ground," so certain forms of cultivated vegetation—such as fruit trees—would not continue to survive as well without man's care.

If the third day of Creation were billions of years long, as evolutionists teach, these plants would have quickly died with no physical

sun to allow photosynthesis (day four) and no insects to pollinate (day six).

God not only spoke of His vegetative creation in Genesis, but He made man so interdependent on vegetation that the entire Bible is filled with references about how we should coexist with plants. This relationship is not limited to the Bible's communication with mankind in an agricultural society, but is today every bit as important as it was when it was initially written.

At the end of the third day of Creation, the Earth was still lighted with a supernatural light. It had no sun, moon, or stars and no reason to rotate, therefore, no time.

Darwin should have been familiar with the biblical story of Creation, as a former seminary student, but in reveling in his freedom from his domineering father and the excitement of the independence of "academic enlightenment," he seems to have been blinded to the truth. "For although they knew God, they did not honor Him as God or give thanks to Him, but they became futile in their thinking, and their foolish hearts were darkened" (Romans 1:21). (See this book's Forward for more details.)

---

1 *ESV Study Bible*, footnotes Genesis 6:17, (Wheaton, IL: Crossway Bibles), 2007, 62
2 "Growth of Reptiles," *Encyclopaedia Britannica* on line, accessed October 30, 2014.

CHAPTER 13

Day Four of Creation, the Universe and Time

In view of such harmony in the cosmos which I, with my limited human mind, am able to recognize, there are yet people who say there is no God. But what makes me really angry is that they quote me for support of such views. Albert Einstein, 1941, 204

HERE IS WHAT HAPPENED ON the fourth day of Creation, as described in Genesis 1:14–19:

> And God said, "Let there be lights in the expanse of the heavens to separate the day from the night. And let them be for signs and for seasons, and for days and years, and let them be lights in the expanse of the heavens to give light upon the earth." And it was so. And God made the two great lights—the greater light to rule the day and the lesser light to rule the night—and the stars. And God set them in the expanse of the heavens to give light on the earth, to rule over the day and over the night, and to separate the light from the darkness. And God saw that it was good. And there was evening and there was morning, the fourth day.

God provided for the measurement of time, as defined by the rotation of the earth, for the first time in day three, using the movement of the sun and stars. Genesis 1:14 says that the purpose of the lights was *to separate the day from the night*, and *to be for signs and for seasons and for days and years*, and for light—all for the benefit of His animal and vegetation Creation. So for the first time, God created a way to count seasons, days, and years.

Psalms 104:19–20 says that God "made the moon to mark the seasons; the sun knows its time for setting. You make darkness, and it is night." God says in Genesis 1:18 that this part of His Creation was good, presumably since these lights function to serve His higher Creation, the organic environment of the earth.

This stated purpose of the creation of the heavens speaks to the futility of man's obsession with discovering life outside of the earth. Jeremiah 10:2 says, "Learn not the way of the nations, nor be dismayed at the signs of the heavens because the nations are dismayed at them."

Jeremiah 31:35–37 explains it this way:

> Thus says the Lord, Who gives the sun for light by day and the fixed order of the moon and the stars for light by night. "If this fixed order departs from before Me, declares the Lord, then shall the offspring of Israel cease from being a nation before Me forever." Thus says the Lord: "If the heavens above can be measured, and the foundations of the earth below can be explored, then I will cast off all the offspring of Israel for all that they have done, declares the Lord."

Jeremiah 33:25–26 says, "Thus says the Lord: 'If I have not established My covenant with day and night and the fixed order of heaven and earth, then I will reject the offspring of Jacob and David My servant.'"

The purpose of the heavens was to sustain man and provide a natural revelation of God's truth. Psalms 148:1–6 says the following:

> Praise the Lord! Praise the Lord from the heavens; praise Him in the heights! Praise Him all His angels; praise Him, all His hosts! Praise Him, sun and moon, praise Him, all you shining stars! Praise Him, you highest heavens, and you waters above the heavens! Let them praise the name of the Lord! For He commanded and they were created. And He established them forever and ever; He gave a decree, and it shall not pass away.

Before this fourth day, there was nothing to differentiate between *days* and *years*—no sun to measure a twenty-four-hour day, a three-month season, or a year.

In the spiritual world, there is no sun or other means of measuring time. In fact, Psalms 90:4 says about God that "a thousand years in Your sight are but as yesterday when it is past, or as a watch in the night," and 2 Peter 3:8 says that "with the Lord one day is as a thousand years, and a thousand years as one day." Job 36:26 says, "Behold, God is great, and we know Him not; the number of His years is unsearchable."

The absence of spiritual time also calls to question the length of time of the first three days of Creation, since there was no way to measure time without a sun. Many Christian evolutionists argue that the Hebrew word translated "day," in Genesis, can mean an era, daylight, or a twenty-four-hour day. Indeed, the Hebrew word *yom* can be found translated in the Bible as "day" to indicate all of these meanings.

But the weakness of this theological evolutionary argument is that the words "the evening and the morning," used for all six days of creation, are not used elsewhere in the Bible for any meaning other than the end and beginning of a twenty-four-hour day. (A study of *Strong's Exhaustive Concordance* shows that "evening" is used for the end of **a twenty-four**-hour day in all fifty-two times in the Old Testament that the word is used and in all seven times in the New Testament that the word is used. Likewise, morning is used in the Bible for the beginning of **a twenty-four**-hour day all 207 times it is found in the Old Testament and all seventeen times it is found in the New Testament.)

We have read that Genesis 1 states that Creation lasted six days with mornings and evenings, and, in addition, Exodus 20:11 states, "For in six days the Lord made heaven and earth, the sea, and all that is in them, and rested on the seventh day. Therefore the Lord blessed the Sabbath day and made it holy." This passage, as well as the context expressed in verses 8–10 of Exodus 20, clearly describes six twenty-four-hour days. God made His Creation for humans, and He could have done it as quickly or as slowly as He wished, but as in all passages of the Bible, He teaches us something with every action and miracle He accomplishes. In the case of the six days of Creation, He invented and taught us natural order, physics, chemistry, biology, botany, geology, astronomy, and all of the other sciences.

One theory of time, during at least the first two days, is that in accordance with Einstein's Theory of Relativity ($E=mc^2$, where E is energy, m is mass, and c is the speed of light) Creation, requiring infinite energy to produce mass from nothing with an initially small mass (the earth), would cause the speed of light to begin infinitely fast.

An infinitely fast speed of light would explain the apparent age of the universe and the large number of light years it spans, and it would allow a vision into the past, during the start of that third day. The past and the present would coexist with no time.

The infinitely large mass of the entire universe, after the fourth day of creation, along with a continuing large energy, would cause the speed of light to decrease to its current constant rate of 186,282 miles per second, since infinite energy keeps mass moving without further creation.

At this relatively slow speed of light, we seem to see objects in the universe that existed millions or billions of years ago. But in the third day of Creation, unlike all subsequent days, the infinitely fast speed of light would have allowed the sight of these far away objects to travel to the earth immediately.

Other theories for flexible time during the first two days of Creation include the following:[1]

- The Burgess model, which describes a rapid aging process for stars and a faster speed of light.[2]

- The Humphreys model, which theorizes that clocks in the cosmos ran about one trillion times faster than those on earth during the Creation Week.[3]
- The Setterfield and Norman model[4] and the Harris[5] model of c decay, which again theorize that the speed of light more gradually slowed, again about a trillion times, but after Creation Week.

Thus, the breadth of the universe is indeed billions of our current light years across, but the actual age of the universe from the fourth day to the present may be only in the thousands of years, as the Bible insinuates. Only God can tell us whether Einstein's theory is true and how it might vary through distant space and into the ancient past, but man has yet to disprove the theory. **Also, only God can know whether these first days were very long or lasted only the twenty-four hours of our "sun days." Why does it matter to us, unless we want to be God—or to be smarter than God—like Adam and Eve?**

If we really believe in an omnipotent God, we must accept that He could have spoken the universe into existence in six days or six seconds. Revelation 4:11 says, "for You created all things, and by Your will they existed, and were [not 'are'] created."

Another possibility is that God created the universe with apparent age, just as He did the seed-yielding plants and fruit-bearing trees.

---

1 Dr. John Harnett, *Starlight, Time and the New Physics* (Eight Mile Plains, Australia: Creation Book Publishers, 2007), 20-28.
2 S. Burgess, *He made the stars also* (Surrey: Day One Publications, 2001).
3 D. R. Humphreys, "New Vistas of Space and Time," *Journal of Creation*, 12, no. 2, (1998), 195-212.
4 T. Norman and B. Setterfield, *The Atomic Constants, Light, and Time* (Menlo Park: SRI International Invited Research, 1986).
5 D. M. Harris, "A Solution to Seeing Stars," *Creation Research Society Quarterly* (September 1978), 112-115.

CHAPTER 14
Day Five of Creation, Aquatic Life and Birds

§

Everyone who is seriously involved in the pursuit of science becomes convinced that a spirit is manifest in the laws of the universe, one that is vastly superior to that of man... In this way the pursuit of science leads to a religious feeling of a special sort, which is indeed quite different from the religiosity of someone more naïve. Albert Einstein, 1936, 202

ON THE FIFTH DAY OF Creation (Genesis 1:20–23), God created living creatures for the first time in the water and the air:

> And God said, "Let the waters swarm with swarms of living creatures, and let birds fly above the earth across the expanse of the heavens." So God created the great sea creatures and every living creature that moves, with which the waters swarm, according to their kinds, and every winged bird according to its kind. And God saw that it was good. And God blessed them, saying, "Be fruitful and multiply and fill the waters in the seas, and let birds multiply on the earth." And there was evening and there was morning, the fifth day.

It should be noted that before day five, when animals were first created, Genesis 1 does not mention the word *living*, even for plants, but beginning in verse 20—the start of the fifth day—*living* or *life* is used to describe fish (verses 20 and 21), animals (verse 24), insects (verse 30), and man (Genesis 2:7). See also 1 Corinthians 15:45: "Thus it is written 'The first man Adam became a living being; the last Adam became a life-giving spirit.'"

For the first time, in day five, God introduces the concept of *kinds*. This term is apparently not the same as *species* in today's scientific usage. Species is a classification of plants or animals having similar characteristics and called by a common name. There are many more *species* than *kinds*. **This differentiation accounts for microevolution, changes within a kind that, in many cases, will form a new species. Microevolution happens so fast that it can be observed and is most of the scientific basis of Darwin's theory.** Dogs evolved from wolves—a poodle much farther than a Siberian Husky—but all of the same *kind*. Some microevolution hits a dead end—as in the case of a mule, the sterile offspring of a male donkey and a mare. There are many other examples of microevolution between *species* but no examples of macroevolution between *kinds*.

For the first time, in verse 22, God blessed His Creation and said to the animals, "Be fruitful and multiply and fill the waters in the seas, and let birds multiply on the earth." There is no concern in God's mind about overpopulation of animals or of extinction of species, nor should there be in our minds. God knew during Creation how we would use and abuse our planet. To prevent abuse He has trusted us with "dominion over the fish of the sea and over the birds of the heavens and over the livestock and over all the earth and over every creeping thing that creeps on the earth" (Genesis 1:26).

As with vegetation in day three—and later, in day six, animals and humans—God created fish and birds with apparent age (they could "swarm") and not as stationary eggs.

Science recognizes inorganics, nonliving organics (such as oil and gas), and living organics (such as plants and animals), but God describes *living* animals as a higher level of organics than plants. **The theory of evolution has difficulty with the origin and interrelation of plant and animal life, but both God and science are clear on the differentiation between these parts of Creation.**

CHAPTER 15

Day Six of Creation, Animals and Humans

§

What is the meaning of human life, or for that matter, of the life of any creature? To know an answer to this question means to be religious. You ask: Does it make any sense, then, to pose this question? I answer: The man who regards his own life and that of his fellow creatures as meaningless is not merely unhappy but hardly fit for life. Albert Einstein, 1934, 202

THE SIXTH DAY BROUGHT ABOUT the creation of living creatures according to their kinds on the earth, including domestic animals (livestock), creeping things (a better translation is *ground crawlers*), and wild animals (beasts). Genesis 1: 24–25 says this:

> And God said "Let the earth bring forth living creatures according to their kinds—livestock and creeping things and beasts of the earth according to their kinds." And it was so. And God made the beasts of the earth according to their kinds and the livestock according to their kinds, and everything that creeps on the ground according to its kind. And God saw that it was good.

Note the different order of verses 24 and 25. In verse 24 the order is livestock, creeping things, beasts; in verse 25 it is beasts, livestock, creeping things. **In other words, they were made simultaneously, not with evolution's assumed order. All animals were made in unique *kinds*, separated forever from other *kinds*, not evolved from them or into them.** God used the word *kinds* five times in day six and twice in day five. His repetition is not accidental; it is significant in our understanding of reality.

The Hebrew word *chay*, translated "living," is not used for plants, only for sea, air, and land animals.[1] Note that God made livestock as separate creatures from the beasts of the earth, rather than domestic animals evolving from, or being tamed from, wild beasts. Psalms 104:30 says that when God sent forth His Spirit, they (all creatures) were created, and God renewed the face of the earth. (See also Deuteronomy 4:32, Job 10:8–11, Psalms 100:3, Ecclesiastes 11:5, Isaiah 45: 12, and Jeremiah 27:5.)

There was no "survival of the fittest" between these animals; all initially survived because God saw it was good, and death would not be good.

In that same sixth day, in Genesis 1:26, God said, "Let Us make man in Our image, after Our likeness. And let them have dominion over the fish of the sea and over the birds of the heavens and over…every creeping thing that creeps on the earth." God states that He created "man in Our [plural] image, after Our likeness." Similar language is found in Genesis 5:1 ("when God created man, He made him in the likeness of God") and in Genesis 9:6b "for God made man in His own image." This is the first of Creation to bear God's image and likeness. Theologians have debated the meaning of God's *image* and *likeness* for thousands of years. Apparently, when we see God in heaven, He will be shaped like a human, as was Jesus on this earth. But we, as Christians, also house the Holy Spirit in our bodily temples, so that presence of God within us seems to make us in the image and likeness of God. In our regenerated souls, we may well have several spiritual senses, as we have five natural senses in our natural bodies.

One of mankind's purposes, according to Genesis 1:26, was to have dominion over all of the lower animal *kinds*. They were created to provide food for humans and to help with work, and to preserve this mutually beneficial relationship, humans are supposed to preserve the lower animals.

Man was made last of all the creatures, so it could not be said that man was in any way a helper to God in Creation. But it was a perfect position for man's existence, since the earth was completely ready for his sustenance and survival.

This creation of man, according to the Bible, did not happen accidentally after billions of years of evolution, but each man was, and still is, planned by God before the foundations of the earth. Isaiah 44:2 (and 44:24) says, "Thus says the Lord Who made you, Who formed you from the womb," and Jeremiah 1:5 says, "Before I formed you in the womb I knew you, and before you were born I consecrated you." (Also see Psalm 71:6 and Galatians 1:15.)

God formed Adam as a mature man from dust "from the ground and breathed into his nostrils the breath of life, and the man became a living creature" (Genesis 2:7). Then "God caused a deep sleep to fall upon the man, and while he slept took one of his ribs and closed up its place with flesh." (This is a record of the first operation—a spiritual one that God performed on His natural Creation.) "And the rib that the Lord God had taken from the man He made into a woman and brought her to the man" (Genesis 2:21–22). The Hebrew word *tesla* is translated elsewhere in the Bible as "side," which would contain not only bone, but muscle and other tissue, and that is probably why Adam said in Genesis 2:23, "This at last is bone of my bones and flesh of my flesh." **Adam and Eve were therefore created with apparent age, just as the plants yielding seed and the trees bearing fruit of Genesis 1:12.**

Genesis 1:27 says that God created man as *male and female*. (See also Genesis 2:18, 5:2, and Matthew 19:4.) In 1 Corinthians 11:8, Paul says, "For man was not made from woman, but woman from man." It is clear in this verse, as in many others, that Paul believed the words of Genesis literally, specifically Genesis 2:18–20: "Then the Lord God said, 'It is not good that the man should be alone; I will make him a helper fit for him.'

Now out of the ground the Lord God had formed every beast of the field and every bird of the heavens...But for Adam there was not found a helper fit for him." God created man and woman sequentially, just as He created all inorganics and organics sequentially by His Word.

Verse 29 says: "And God said, 'Behold, I have given you every plant yielding seed that is on the face of all the earth, and every tree with seed in its fruit. You shall have them for food." He again explains in verse 30 that these green plants were also provided to the land animals for food.

This ultimate creation of humans provided a new birth of creatures. For the first time, in verse 31, the Creation is described as *very good*, in God's image, after His likeness (verse 27), with the expressed responsibilities (verse 28) of procreating to fill the earth and of subduing and having dominion over it. God has given His children governance over all of His Creation including our own bodies, which he says are the temple of the Holy Spirit. (See 1 Corinthians 3: 16–17, 6:19, and Ephesians 2:22.)

Summary of Creation

During these six days of Creation, God has proceeded more logically—from a chemical prospective—than any evolutionist. He explained Creation starting with the basic inorganic molecules of water and those composing the core of the earth, which were formed supernaturally from nothing. Remember that the supernatural realm has no chemistry, laws, or limitations. He then created order and separation, followed by the *dry land earth*. Next He created plants and fruit trees with age, yielding seed. So this vegetation was mature—with created age—just as other parts of creation were, such as water, rocks, minerals, animals, and humans. God, miraculously, can create what He wishes. He is not constrained by science or nature in His creation. If He can create a human, He would logically not create it as a newborn infant, unable to survive on its own. It would have to have some age. Likewise, a rock could be created at any time in its natural formation stages, in order to achieve its very purpose of creation: to support humanity. If the freshly created human or rock were scientifically tested, it would show age.

Thus far in day three, there is no sun, moon, or universe; therefore, there is no rotation of the earth and no time. God makes it clear that, at this point in history, time began in the fourth day with the creation of the rest of the universe. Because plants could not have existed for long without photosynthesis from the sun and pollination from insects, in order to accept evolution as truth, the order of Creation, as presented in the Bible, would have to be changed so the creation of the sun and the creation of insects preceded that of vegetation. The supernaturally created light could have provided photosynthesis but not pollination.

That was Darwin's main failure and the source of his folly. A supernatural God is a God of miracles, and miracles, being supernatural, do not obey our natural rules. We must admit that God could have created everything by His word out of nothing—in less than one second and in any order He wished. But in His wisdom, love, and understanding of our weaknesses, He describes Creation in very logical steps that we can fathom and believe with our simplistic minds.

As in the entire Old Testament, God had a more important message to communicate in Creation than to confirm science. Genesis 1 is a prophesy and explanation of Jesus—as is the entire Old Testament. Jesus revealed the mystery of God's complete truth, a new covenant, revealed in part to Daniel (Daniel 2:28). Colossians 1:26 describes the new covenant as "the mystery hidden for ages and generations but now revealed to His saints." And John 1:1 explains, "In the beginning was the Word" (John 1:1). Jesus was the Word and was God. God used the Word, both Jesus and the divine expression of speech, to create the universe and also to create the scriptures.

The order of Creation predicts the building blocks of molecular chemistry: water, light, air, inorganics, organic vegetation, organic animals, and nonliving hydrocarbon organics. "Chemistry is the study of the composition of matter and the changes that matter undergoes. Because living and nonliving things are made of matter, chemistry affects all aspects of life and most natural events."[2] Pure water contains only hydrogen and oxygen, one of only two substances with this particular combination. (The other is hydrogen peroxide.) Air now consisted of nitrogen, oxygen, carbon dioxide, argon, other minor gases, and water vapor. Air only contains about 0.00005 percent hydrogen;[3] therefore, would not be able to produce hydrocarbons with carbon from carbon dioxide (0.04 percent)—just as the hydrogen and oxygen in air will not combine to form water without external heat and the resultant explosion.

Therefore, on day three, God used the more chemically efficient method of producing hydrocarbons that we find continuing today. He created vegetation that produces carbon, which combines with the hydrogen in water to continue the production of vegetation and animals for the sustenance of humans (Genesis 1:30, 2:9).

On day four God created the sun and the rest of the universe for the expressed purpose of giving light and for separating the day and the night, for signs and for seasons and for days and years (Genesis 1:14). The universe is for us, to give us the gift of time and natural revelation, not to grow alien civilizations. There are no God-given restrictions for using the rest of the universe for our resources and space. Why be concerned with the "population explosion"? God has provided for that.

Day five brought the creation of sea creatures and birds, again for the purpose of human sustenance (Genesis 9:2–3). These animals—along with domestic and wild animals and humans that were created in day six—contain ever more complex DNA, as is chemically logical. Even though God is not restricted by chemistry, He has given us chemistry and the other sciences, which have not been developed by humans but only discovered by humans. Virtually all of the earlier scientists, even through Einstein, recognized this as fact, but this point has been lost in the confusion present in the minds of some of the more outspoken scientists in recent times. **The wonderful balance and organization of the sciences, as evidenced by God's Creation, cannot have resulted from chance, as explained in the law of entropy and by statistics.**

Darwin's lack of understanding of the supernatural has been passed on to theologians and scientists of recent time, who have attempted to explain the scientific "weakness" of the twenty-four-hour day creation theory as myth or a literary framework. They ignore the fact that there was no measurement of time during the first two-plus days. Time was irrelevant; it did not exist. God called these two days, "days," but in the supernatural realm of a nonspinning earth without a supporting universe of sunlight and gravity, there was no such thing as a day, as we define it. These were God's days and 2 Peter 3:8 says, "But do not overlook this one fact, beloved, that with the Lord one day is as a thousand years, and a thousand years as on day." (Also see Psalms 90:4.) But starting in day four, time was created. See chapter 11 for a detailed discussion on the length of days during Creation. In summary, God could have used any period of time He wished for Creation.

God continues His explanation with the increasingly complex organics being created: vegetative organics in day three, fish and birds—as animal organics—in day five, and more complex animals, and, finally, humans in day six. These last days of Creation, as described by God, obviously preceded all evolutionary literature and provided evolutionists with a structure on which to base their theory that God was not involved. **Evolution has no purpose except to deny God.**

Darwinism provides an explanation of how our imagination can stretch three or four days of written history into billions of years. (Darwin started at day three.) The only logical purpose of this theory is to let random chance displace God so that we can be God ourselves. Granted, billions of years do not explain evolution, but the concept serves to boggle our little minds to the point of acceptance.

Contrary to Darwin and all other evolutionary theories, God has clearly communicated a logical sequence of spiritual and natural events that explain, supernaturally and naturally, exactly how our universe was formed. With this background and understanding, we can further explore God's Word to determine the future of species.

---

1 Henry M. Morris III, *Your Origins Matter* (Dallas, TX: Institute for Creation Research, 2013), 18.
2 Wilbraham, Staley, Matta, and Waterman, *Chemistry* (Boston, Mass: Prentice Hall, 2005, 7).
3 Ibid, R4.

Part 3
The Origin through Evolution

CHAPTER 16

Introduction

*A religious person is devout in the sense that he has
no doubt about the significance of those superpersonal
objects and goals that neither require nor are capable
of rational foundation. Albert Einstein, 1940, 203*

FROM A NATURAL PERSPECTIVE, THE evolutionary view of the origin of the universe and the future of species is the only "logical" solution, since it is the only thought process explainable by natural theories or laws. Alvin Plantinga says, "Human ingenuity is nearly limitless: almost anything can be explained in one way or another."[1] **Natural logic fails at its interface with the supernatural or spiritual. So we should critically examine the evolutionary explanations to see if they pass the test of scientific law or whether they are just theoretical science.** Theoretical science, in the same way as theoretical thinking, has no bounds, no rules, and no laws—nor should it. The results are simply science fiction, entertaining, interesting, and perhaps stimulating, but still unproven theory and not science.

There is beautiful logic in the rules for a scientific law; that it must be observed, documented, and be repeatable by others. In other words, the goal of a scientific law is to determine a scientific truth

beyond the figment of someone's imagination, which has been seen and can be seen by others.

In order to retain scientific credibility, this part of the book will describe evolutionary explanations—even if only theories—but, other than quotes, will limit naturalistic conclusions to science and not theory. Previous chapters have explained popular evolutionary theory as invented by others. If a theory is proven true, it will become law. If it is not proven true—because it did not meet the criteria of being successfully observed, documented, and repeatable—it should be discarded in our search for the proven truth.

There are relatively few laws of chemistry; Wikipedia lists fourteen. Because of the subject of this book, we will mostly concentrate our scientific studies on chemistry, which Raymond Chang defines as "the study of matter and the changes it undergoes" in his chemistry textbook.[2] Chemistry is also known as the central science since it bridges the other natural sciences.[3]

Two basic scientific laws that especially relate to our study of evolution are these:

- *The Conservation of Mass*—Mass can be changed, but it can neither be created nor destroyed.
- *Entropy*—There is a net loss of energy with time in a closed system. Mechanically, entropy indicates a natural disorder (i.e., if you cut a dictionary into letter-sized pieces and throw them into the air, there is virtually no statistical possibility of the pieces falling to earth in the original order and form).

---

1 Alvin Plantinga, *Evolution, Neutrality, and Antecedent Probability: a Reply to Van Till and McMullen* (Notre Dame, IN: Calvin Library of Christian Philosophy, 1991)38 of 45.
2 Raymond Chang, *Chemistry*, 9th edition (McGraw Hill, 2007, accessed on line, October 30,2014.
3 Brown, Lemay, Burnsten and Lemay, *Chemistry, The Central Science*, 8th edition (Prentice Hall, 1999), Accessed on line, October 30, 2014.

CHAPTER 17
The Beginning of Natural Reality

Scientific research can reduce superstition by encouraging people to think and view things in terms of cause and effect. It is certain that a conviction akin to a religious feeling, of the rationality or intelligibility of the world lies behind all scientific work of a higher order. Albert Einstein, 1922, 194

SINCE MATTER CANNOT BE CREATED, and natural reality does not include a supernatural entity such as God, some natural substances must have existed forever. Without a beginning, reality would not include a dimension or concept of time, at least before the sun and the earth were formed and we were able to measure the passage of time. Before that formation, there may have been theoretical time, but since it was not observed, it would not have been scientific. Likewise, any development of natural inorganics or organics could not have occurred from nothing, in accordance with the law of conservation of mass, and even if matter had popped into existence from nonmatter, the transformation was not observed; therefore, that possibility remains a theory and not science.

If there is a supernatural reality, there has to be a god, and that god has to be real. (See chapter 5.) As such, the scientific method—as described in the Creation story—is confirmed, God having observed Creation and recorded it. It is only unconfirmed in the third test: that it is repeatable.

But, as explained in chapter 32, there will be another creation of the New Heaven and the New Earth.

Mankind has spent billions of dollars trying to create life from something simpler and has, thus far, failed because that third test of a scientific law is limited to natural reality. Humans cannot repeat a supernatural event. Therefore, true science, in its wisdom, and true scientists, such as Darwin and Teilhard, have ignored the theory of existence from nonexistence as fantasy and have concentrated on evolution beyond Creation. Indeed scientists such as H. C. Dudley, professor of radiation physics at the University of Illinois Medical Center, **state that "finally, by 1875 this concept of spontaneous generation resulting purely from the lack of information, was laid to rest."**[1] One of the reasons for this conclusion was that in 1860 Pasteur conducted experiments just a year after the publication of *The Origin of Species* that demonstrated the fallacy of spontaneous generation.[2]

The Big Bang Theory

The big bang theory has evolved from work by Georges Henri Joseph Edouard Lemaitre in 1927, Edwin Hubble in 1928, Arno Penzias and Robert Wilson in 1964, and Stephen Hawking, George Ellis, and Roger Penrose in 1968 and 1970 into the prevailing cosmological theory of the beginning of the universe and time. The theory suggests that around fourteen billion years ago, an explosion of unknown origin caused a dense mass of unknown origin to rapidly expand forming subatomic particles, atoms, clouds of elements, stars, and galaxies.

The law of entropy has been used to justify the big bang theory, with scientists explaining that since evidence shows that the universe is deteriorating into chaos, there must have been a beginning. Davies states the following:

> During the big bang, huge quantities of energy were available to cause the incoherent production of vast matter and antimatter. Eventually, much cooled, this material would have aggregated into

stars and planets. **Unfortunately there is a major snag with this simple idea. When antimatter encounters matter, the two annihilate each other with a violent release of energy—the reverse process of matter creation.**[3]

The big bang theory is a form of theistic evolution, one of the beliefs discussed in chapter 6, that allows an acceptance of a creator God Who is no longer involved in nature and reality. Some Christians still believe in the big bang theory but believe that God has been involved since the formation of the earth; while some believe that God came back into the picture only when primates were evolved enough to accept a soul. Regardless, these beliefs do not coincide with God's words in the historical book of Genesis.

One of the most controversial issues concerning the big bang theory is the logical presumption that the universe, including matter and space, would be ever expanding three dimensionally with an outside spherical edge. It follows that there must be a point of origin from which matter and space move because of the energy the bang imparted to them. This movement can be accelerating, decelerating, regular, or irregular, depending on the interpretation or theory.

This confusion leads to many questions, such as these:

- Was all matter initially formed, or is matter continuing to appear from nothing?
- Does this leave a vacuum at the site of the big bang? If not, what kept some matter from moving?
- What is beyond the expanded edge of the universe?
- If the center of the universe is elsewhere, the matter on our side would be moving with us, and that on the opposite side, away from us—and that at ninety degrees from us in that direction. Why hasn't this differentiation been reported?
- In a vacuum, all matter—regardless of size or density—will move at the same speed but all in its own unique direction radial to the point of origin. Why hasn't this been observed?

I am a practical scientist and engineer, and certainly not a theoretical scientist, but even I can theorize answers to these questions and explanations of these statements. But just like those ideas now being considered and even believed, there are fatal holes in all theories to date. The one irrefutable theory is that God supernaturally created the universe by His word alone—that He created it "good" and for His ultimate purpose of Creation: humankind. **This theory has no holes, but it requires a belief in a limitless supernatural power. It is very difficult for people who have been trained to think that they can understand everything to accept this belief. Believe me; I've been there, but God has seen me through.**

THE CENTER OF THE UNIVERSE

The big bang theory requires space and all of the matter in space to have originated at one point, which would be the center of the universe. After the "bang" the matter and space would move or expand outward. Hubble[4] observed galaxies moving away from him in all directions with speeds in proportion to their distance.[5] He said, "This would imply that we occupy a unique position in the universe…such a favored position, of course, is intolerable.[6] As a result of this confusion and the philosophical position that many astronomers have taken, some consider that space itself is moving, but the galaxies are fixed in space.

Hubble addressed this problem by assuming that space was curved so that a center and an edge could be avoided. Big Bangers and others who attempt to explain the expanding universe scientifically have vacillated between homogeneity, isotropicy, a spherical universe with a bounded edge, a center and a net gravitational force, an unbounded universe, space-time curvature, a flat universe, and many other unproven theories. George Ellis, the South African cosmologist, said, "What I want to bring into the open is that we are using philosophical criteria in choosing our models. A lot of cosmetology tries to hide that."[7] All of these theories have lethal difficulties since studies such as the *2df Galaxy Redshift Survey* and the *Sloan Digital Sky Survey* show that the universe is isotropic but not homogeneous. The studies indicate that the universe has a unique center, and the earth is somewhere near that center.[8]

God said He made the stars and "set them in the expanse of the heavens" (Genesis 1: 16–17). God numbered the stars "as the sand that is on the seashore" (Genesis 22:17). He "determines the number of the stars" and He "gives to all of them names" (Psalms 147:4). **If Creation is a supernatural event and God did as He said and created the universe to serve humans, it is logical that the earth would indeed be in the center of His Creation, as science shows, regardless of how "intolerable" that is to some cosmologists.** The very fact according to Hubble—that the universe is expanding on all sides away from the earth—puts the earth in the center of the universe and, therefore, at the center of creation. If this is true, the Creation story is the most logical explanation for the universe.

The Origin of the Universe
Paul Davies summarizes the frustration of evolutionists as follows:

> Any system of thought which claims to provide an understanding of the physical world must make some statement about the origin of the world. At its most basic, the choice is stark. **Either the universe has already existed (in one form or another) or it began, more or less abruptly, at some particular moment in the past. Both alternatives have long been a source of perplexity to theologians, philosophers, and scientists, and both present obvious difficulties for the layman.**[9]

Stephen Hawking, in his confusion, was unable to fathom Davies's logic, and in *The Grand Design*, he makes this statement:

> The laws of gravity and quantum theory explain how something comes from nothing. But gravity cannot be defined without mass, and quantum theory accounts for certain interactions between energy and matter. Both have demonstrated value for understanding how existing things function; neither has obvious value to account

for the origin of those things...**If there had ever been a time when absolutely nothing existed, nothing would exist now.**[10]

This is why all serious proponents of evolution, including Darwin and Teilhard, start with God and Creation. Even Hazen and Davies leave open the possibility of Creation. But still, contemporary scientists and educators diverge into imaginary theories that are not consistent with science or with the Creation story of the Bible and other ancient secular traditions.

Francis Schaeffer in *Genesis in Space and Time* had this to say:

> When we read "In the beginning God created the heavens and the earth," we are not left with something hung in a vacuum: Something existed before Creation and that something was personal and not static; The father loved the Son; there was a plan; there was communication; and promises were made prior to the creation of the heavens and the earth.

Here is Schaeffer's conclusion:

> This leads us, of course, to the modern notion of Being. Being is there. But the question immediately rises: "Has it always been there?" This is modern man's basic mystery. Man is shut up to relatively few answers. I think we often fail to understand that the deeper we go into study at this point, the simpler the alternatives become. In almost any profound question, the number of final possibilities is very few indeed. Here are four; **(1) Once there was absolutely nothing and now there is something, (2) Everything began with an impersonal something, (3) Everything began with a personal something, and (4) There is and always has been a dualism.**[11]

The Distance to Stars

Astronomy has proven that the distance to the most remote point in the universe is many light years away. This means that at the speed of light, it will take many years for the light from these stars to reach earth. Therefore, many scientists reason, the universe has to be at least millions of years old. There are at least two fairly simple reasons for this confusion:

- Since God created plants, animals, and humans with apparent age (see chapters 12, 14, and 15), it is consistent that He would create the universe with apparent age. **Therefore, on that fourth day of Creation, all of the millions of light years of the universe's breadth were created with light reaching the earth.**
- Einstein's theory of relativity, $E=mc^2$, indicates that an infinite energy (E) from the big bang, or from God's Creation, would require an infinite speed of light (c)—especially initially, as explained in chapter 13. **An infinite speed of light would allow the millions of light years at the beginning to pass instantly.**

THE HIGH TEMPERATURE OF THE EARLY EARTH

For the last hundred years, geologists have generally agreed that conditions during the Hadean period, the first geologic eon, were utterly hostile to life. But recent research has concluded that "conditions on earth for the first 500 million years after it formed may have been surprisingly similar to the present day, complete with oceans, continents, and active crystal plates."[12] It seems that, every day, the latest scientific research confirms the story of Creation and confirms the fantasy of evolution.

GEOLOGICAL AGE

Michael Pitman said, **"Fossils are used as the key for placing rocks in geological order. The criterion for assigning fossils to specific places in that chronology is the assumed evolutionary progression of life; the assumed evolutionary progression is based on the** fossil record so constructed. The main evidence for evolution is therefore the assumption of evolution."[13] Fossils are typically dated by the strata of sediment in which they are found. This requires an assumption of uniform deposition with time, even though deposition—by definition—requires flowing water, normally from a flood of some magnitude. The biblical account of Noah's Flood provides a more logical scientific explanation for rapid deposition, as well as the many findings of petrified objects covering multiple geologic ages.

Darwin's evolutionary theory exploded, probably permanently among scientists, in the mid-1980s when over sixty thousand fossil specimens of the Burgess shale rocks from Western Canada were refound. The specimens were discovered by Charles D. Walcott, the director of the Smithsonian Institute in 1909, and were reburied in the drawers of his laboratory. These fossils proved that an explosion of life appeared simultaneously in the Cambrian era, supposedly 530 million years ago; the fossils showed the basic anatomies of all currently existing animals—from sponges to vertebrates. The animals lived in underwater mudbanks and were killed instantaneously by mudslides.[14]

The Age of the Universe

Dust on the Moon

NASA had calculated that the dust on the surface of the moon was several feet deep because of the supposed age of the moon (about five billion years) and because of no wind to blow the dust away. The landing craft was designed to rest on the dust instead of the moon surface. I remember seeing photographs of the July 20, 1969, landing with Neil Armstrong stepping onto the surface. His foot sunk a fraction of an inch, as did the lunar capsule's leg pads. **This mistake indicates that the true age of the moon is a fraction of that calculated.** These photographs are available today on the Internet at NASA.gov. NASA's

LADEE again studied the depth of the dust on the moon in 2013, and no further explanation was found.

Radiocarbon Dating

Cosmic rays in the atmosphere trigger a process that changes nitrogen into C^{14}, which is unstable, and combines with oxygen to produce C^{14} containing carbon dioxide along with the normal C^{12} carbon dioxide. This heavy C^{14} carbon dioxide circulates down through the atmosphere and is ingested by plants. As long as the plants and the animals that eat the plants live, the C^{14}/C^{12} ratio remains constant at the same ratio found in the atmosphere. In today's environment there is about one C^{14} atom per trillion C^{12} atoms. After the organism's death, the decayed C^{14} atoms are not replaced, and the ratio based on the decay rate is used to estimate the length of time since death. This decay rate slows as the number of C^{14} atoms decreases and is calculated as a half-life (the time it takes to decrease by 50 percent), of 5,730 years. Using this knowledge, scientists—by making several assumptions—are able to calculate the age of a carbon-containing sample. **Many known ages have been erroneously dated by using this method, which has led researchers to question its accuracy. For example, the minimum detection limit for instrumentation today is about eighteen half-lives, or 103,000 years, much less than the age many samples have been dated.**[15][16]

Also, the sample must have been saturated with C^{14} when the organic containing the atom died. Living organisms continually ingest carbon throughout their lifetimes. There is no assurance that this saturation occurred for every organic. Tests of unsaturated samples would show greater ages than the samples' actual ages. In addition, the half-life must remain constant throughout the time, again with no proof or assurance. These questions of assumption accuracy are necessary since there are so many examples of major discrepancies in carbon dating and between carbon dating and dating with other heavier isotopes.

The simple answer for a creationist to this dating dilemma is that God created, according to Genesis, plants, animals, and man with apparent age (plants bearing seed, trees containing fruit, animals and humans able to function on their own), so it is consistent that inorganics such as rocks—and even the entire universe—would have also been created with apparent age, even millions of years, in order to be able to function initially to support mankind.

Radioisotope Dating

Brian Thomas and John Morris said, "Geologists do not directly measure the age of a rock. They choose rocks containing radioactive 'parent' isotopes that emit particles and radiation to become a different 'daughter' element and measure ratios of elements to their isotopes."[17]

The inaccuracy of radioisotope dating was obvious when the fresh lava dome at Mount St. Helens, which was ten years old, was dated at 340,000 years old using radioisotope methods. The old "uniformitarian" theory, that nuclear decay has always been constant since the formation of the earth or the universe, has caused numerable cases of misdating known origins of rocks.

Biblical Dating of the Universe

This section is included to provide a contrast between evolution's assumption that the universe is billions of years old and Bishop Ussher's calculations from the Bible that the earth was created in 4004 BC. Studies of ancient civilizations that produced literature of some kind include the Chinese (as long ago as about 3400 BC), Egyptians (at about 3110 BC), Babylonians (at about 3300 BC), and the Jewish calendar at about 3762 BC.[18] In 2002 Kurt P. Wise calculated biblically that there were 1,656 years between Creation and Noah's Flood. This would mean that, biblically, Creation occurred at least five thousand years ago, assuming that these civilizations began after the flood.[19]

So most biblical and historical evidence of the age of the universe and its civilizations point to a Creation that happened between five thousand and seven thousand years ago. This is a radical difference in age compared to evolutionary estimates, which are only explained by presuppositions or assumptions.

---

1 H. C. Dudley, *The Unsettled Earth* (Ann Arbor, MI: Ann Arbor Science, 1975) 67.
2 Michael Pitman, *Adam and Evolution, A Scientific Critique of Neo-Darwinism* (Grand Rapids, MI: Baker Book House, 1984) 47.
3 Paul Davies, *God and the New Physics* (New York: Simon & Schuster, 1983) 28.
4 John Hartnett, *Starlight, Time and the New Physics* (Australia: Creation Book Publishers, 2007)74.

5 Hartnett, *Starlight, Time and the New Physics,*74.
6 E. Hubble, *The Observational Approach to Cosmotology* (Oxford: Clarendon Press, 1937).

7 George Ellis "Profile: George F. R. Ellis; Thinking Globally, Acting Universally," *Scientific American*, 273 no. 4, 1995273 no. 4, (1995).
8 Hartnett, *Starlight, Time and the New Physics*.
9 Paul Davies, *God and the New Physics*.
10 Rubel Shelly, "Stephen Hawking: design, but no designer?" *The Tennessean*, September 13, 2010.
11 Francis A. Schaeffer, *Genesis in Time and Space* (Glendale, CA: Regal Books and Downers Grove, IL: Intervarsity Press, 1972) 18,19.
12 "Hellishly Hot? Maybe Not," *Vanderbilt Magazine*, (Winter 2015).
13 Michael Pitman, *Adam and Evolution, A Scientific Critique of Neo-Darwinism, 191* .
14 Gerald L. Schroeder, *The Science of God: The Convergence of Scientific and Biblical Wisdom* (Broadway Books, 1998).
15 Kurt P. Wise, *Faith, Form and Time* (Nashville: Broadman & Holman, 2002) 67.
16 Jake Herbert, "Rethinking Carbon 14 Dating," *Acts & Facts* (April 2013).
17 Brian Thomas and John Morris, "Doesn't Radioisotope Dating Prove Rocks are Millions of Years Old?" *Acts & Facts* (February 2013).
18 Dorothy Allford, MD, *Instant Creation-Not Evolution*, (New Yory, NY: Stein and Day, 1978) 165.
19 Kurt P. Wise, *Faith, Form and Time* (Nashville: Broadman & Holman, 2002) 52.

CHAPTER 18
Chemical Changes, Inorganic to Organic

◊

My intuition was not strong enough in the field of mathematics to differentiate clearly the fundamentally important...from the rest of the more or less dispensable erudition. Also, my interest in the study of nature was no doubt stronger...In this field I soon learned to sniff out that which might lead to fundamentals and to turn aside...from the multitude of things that clutter up the mind and divert from the essentials. Albert Einstein, 1949, 17

THE CHEMICAL COMPLEXITY OF MATTER begins with atoms and progresses to elements, inorganic molecules and compounds, and organic compounds. All organics are—or contain—hydrocarbons, which have at least one carbon and several hydrogen atoms. Inorganic carbon compounds such as cyanide (CN), carbon monoxide (CO), carbon dioxide (CO_2), carbides and carbonic acid (H_2CO_3) do not meet this definition; the acid completely breaks down in water.

The simplest and most abundant organic compound is methane, which has only one carbon atom. All other organics have one or more carbon atoms and are bonded with inorganics or other organics. We will examine the formation of methane to a limited extent since it is the building block of all organics.

There are only two ways of forming methane naturally: at low depths in the soil, methane forms as a by-product of anaerobic decomposition from the fermentation of organic matter, and thermogenic methane is formed in deeper substrates over time from the heat and pressure of the overlaying soil. Oil is formed at lower temperatures and shallower depths, and methane (natural gas) at higher temperatures and greater depths.[1]

Industrially, methane can be made by hydrogenating carbon dioxide. In the laboratory, CO_2 can be formed by the destructive distillation of acetic acid and soda lime or by aluminum carbide and water or strong acids. Much recent research has been done to develop an inexpensive source of energy for space travel by the hydrogenating of methane from carbon dioxide and hydrogen at high temperatures and/or pressures using catalysts and electricity. But the limitation, much as it was at the beginning of time, is that the hydrogen, the catalysts, and the power must be imported from earth.[2]

The formation of methane requires another organic or carbon dioxide, hydrogen, a catalyst, and electricity. So, in accordance with the Law of Conservation of Mass, methane cannot be produced from nothing.

No science has ever, or will ever, succeed in producing inorganics or organics from nothing, since there is nothing to start with, and the most basic of all scientific laws prohibits that possibility. But there is no scientific or logical prohibition of the supernatural creation of atoms that can combine to form methane or even more complex organics. **The philosophical question, then, must be faced; if a supernatural "miracle" occurred at the beginning of time to form methane from nothing, is it unreasonable to assume that a larger miracle could have produced the universe, life, and humans?** Once a supernatural event is accepted, the order of magnitude is irrelevant. In other words, a miracle is a miracle—regardless of its magnitude—and once you cross the line of accepting *any* miracle or supernatural event, to be consistent you must consider other supernatural events.

---

1 "How methane is formed," "The Sabatier Process," Wikipedia, accessed 10/30/14
2 Ibid.

CHAPTER 19
Chemical Changes, Organic to Living Vegetative Organic

§

In every true searcher of Nature there is a kind of religious reverence, for he finds it impossible to imagine that he is the first to have thought out the exceedingly delicate threads that connect his perceptions. Albert Einstein, 1920, 194

Darwin wisely refused to speculate on the beginnings of organic life and admitted that "To my mind it accords better with what we know of the laws impressed on matter by the Creator."[1] He also had the integrity to ask, "but do they (eminent naturalists of late) believe that at innumerable periods in the earth's history certain elemental atoms have been commanded suddenly to flash into living tissues?"[2]

There is commonality in all matter in that matter consists entirely of molecules. Living organic matter has a further commonality in that it contains the very complex molecules of DNA and RNA, which literally program the living organisms to be plants or animals, to be of a certain species, to have certain inherited characteristics, and to adapt to environmental changes.[3]

Much research work has been done in the last few years to explain the chemical changes from nonliving to living organic matter. In 1924 Alexander Oparin proposed that the spontaneous generation of life that originally occurred was now impossible because of changes in the initial conditions on earth.[4] Oparin's work is still followed in recent research.

In 1987, Robert Shapiro summarized his theories:

- The early earth had a chemically reducing atmosphere.
- This atmosphere, exposed to energy in various forms, produced simple organic compounds (monomers).
- These compounds accumulated in a "soup," which may have been concentrated at various locations.
- By further transformation, more complex organic polymers—and ultimately, life—developed in the soup.[5]

In 1952 the Miller-Urey Experiment used a methane, ammonia, and hydrogen mixture with an electric charge to form amino acid, one of the building blocks of protein.

One of the experimenters with Miller and Urey, J. D. Bernal, wrote in 1967 that "it is not enough to explain the formation of such molecules…(what is necessary)…is a physical-chemical explanation of the origin of these molecules that suggests the presence of suitable sources and sinks for free energy."[6]

Clara Moskowitz stated in 2012 that "life's building blocks may have formed in dust around a young sun."[7]

There is still no standard model of the origin of life. Most are still based on Oparin's theories from 1924.

Current research is attempting to determine if RNA molecules could have been spontaneously formed that were capable of catalyzing their own replication. DNA has been synthesized from virus DNA and from cellular chromosome DNA, but no one has been able to successfully form RNA or DNA from inorganics or nonliving organics. This construction is theoretically possible naturally, but—to date and forever—it will be beyond all but imagination.

The basic unit of both animal and plant structures is a cell. Plant and animal cells differ considerably. Plant cell walls are rigid and nonliving, usually made of some form of cellulose. The living material within a cell, protoplasm, contains the nucleus and the cytoplasm. The protoplast and the nucleus may divide into two chromosomes that sexually reproduce new cells having the DNA of the parent cell.[8] [9] Plant cells also contain chromatophores, which determine the pigments the plant exhibits. The plant DNA determines the formation and growth of things like leaves, blossoms, fruit, roots, and bark, and this complexity points to an external Designer, Whose miracles we cannot duplicate.

Many hypotheses such as these have been proposed over the past ninety years with no success, but the desperate need for an explanation of the origin of life without God allows continued funding of futile experimentation, normally at public expense.

---

1 Charles Darwin, "Recapitulation and Conclusion", *The Origin of Species*,(New York, NY:Bantam Books) 3994.
2 Ibid, 394.
3 E. Roberts Alley, *A Christian Environmentalist* (USA: Xulon Press, 2013) 85.
4 Alexander Oparin, *The Origin of Life*, 1924 (London: Wiedenfield and Nicholson, 1967 translation; New York: Dover, 1952).
5 Robert Shapiro, *Origins: A Skeptic's Guide to the Creation of Life on Earth* (New York, NY: Bantam Books, 1987).
6 J. D. Bernal, *Origins of Life* (London: Wiedenfield and Nicholson, 1969).
7 Clara Moskowitz, Space.Com, 2012.
8 Gainey and Lord, *Microbiology of Water and Sewage* (Englewood Cliffs, NJ: Prentice-Hall, 1952).
9 "Artificial Gene Synthesis," Wikipedia, accessed June 2015.

CHAPTER 20
Chemical Changes, Living Vegetative Organic to Living Animal Organic

Everything is determined...by forces over which we have no control. It is determined for the insect as well as for the star. Human beings, vegetables, or cosmic dust—we all dance to a mysterious tune, intoned in the distance by an invisible piper. Albert Einstein, 1929, 196

DARWIN SAID THAT LIFE INITIALLY was "breathed into a few forms or into one" and that "I should infer from analogy that probably all the organic beings which have ever lived on this earth have descended from some primordial form into which life was first breathed."[1] He, as a few evolutionists have since, wisely accepted that the scientific Law of the Conservation of Mass is true, and he refused to speculate on the origin of what was breathed into. He also had the scientific integrity to not propose that animals evolved from plants, or visa versa, since neither he, nor anyone, can prove that. So there has never been an acceptable theory of that potential step in evolution.

Carol Cleland of the University of Colorado was quoted as saying, "Current attempts to answer the question 'What is life' by defining life in terms of features like metabolism or reproduction—features that we ordinarily use to recognize samples of terrestrial life—are unlikely to succeed."[2]

There has been some effort in recent years to prove that organics evolved from other organics of deep terrestrial origin through synthesis, driven by unknown energy sources (Miller-Utey Experiments) or from extraterrestrial origin from organic molecules in interstellar dust clouds and rained down on planets (pseudo-panspermia).[3]

Robert Hazen says this:

> **I think** the most **compelling** scenario for life's origins is based on the **concept** of emergent complexity. We observe, **over and over**, in nature, when **lots of objects, lots of particles**, like sand grains or stars or molecules, or cells, when they interact, they **tend to yield** structures that are **far more complex**, that have **behaviors that are far beyond** anything that the individual sand grain, or star, or cell, could do itself. This kind of emergent complexity is the **key to understanding** the origin of life. The origin of life was a sequence of emergent steps. First, **lots of small molecules came together to form larger molecular structures**, structures that were able to condense and form structures like cell membranes, and so forth. And then, **some of these molecules actually began to self-replicate—groups of molecules making copies of themselves**, and **growing at the expense of all of the surrounding atoms and molecules** and using energy from the environment. **And ultimately, that self-replicating system, the emergence of that system led to the kind of competition and natural selection that drove the evolution into the first cells and beyond.**[4]

You may be interested in rereading the previous paragraph, considering the scientific validity of the words that I have printed in bold.

Hazen is trained in geology and earth science and teaches earth science at George Mason University. His attempt at fantasizing the truth of cellular evolution from an earth-science education demonstrates the danger in blindly accepting the words of scientists with limited backgrounds.

Wikipedia presents a "Timeline of Evolutionary History" with times in billions of years in the past as follows:

Time Life Form

- 3.6 Simple cells
- 3.4 Cells performing photosynthesis
- 2.0 Complex cells
- 1.2 Sexually reproducing cells
- 0.6 Simple animals
- 0.5 Fish, amphibians
- 0.475 Land plants
- 0.400 Insects
- 0.300 Reptiles
- 0.200 Animals
- 0.150 Birds
- 0.130 Flowers
- 0.060 Primates
- 0.020 Great apes
- 0.0025 Humans
- 0.0002 Modern humans (200,000 years)

Note that the order is different than the order God described in Genesis, as quoted in Genesis chapters 12–15 above.

Evolutionary scientists continue to imagine possibilities of conversion from nothing to inorganic or vegetative origin, but so far the "nothing" imagined has not been discovered. Indeed, a "nothing" cannot be discovered by science, because it is supernatural.

Animal cells are similar to plant cells in that they contain a wall, in this case a living membrane, a nucleus, and cytoplasm. The reproduction process is similar to a plant, with the parent cell passing coded DNA to the reproduced cell. This coded DNA allows the various animal to have living automatic processes, such as respiration, kidneys, temperature control, eyes, brain, instinct, enzymes, the cardiovascular system, liver, gall bladder, skin, sweat glands, and other things needed to function.

Similar to plant cells, but more complex in orders of magnitude, animal coded DNA cannot be explained away by adding millions and billions of years to allow random formations of complex living machinery. A caution is that the rules of chance and statistics must recalibrate odds at every trial. In other words, if the odds are one-to-ten that something will happen in an event, when the event is repeated a second time, the odds are still one-to-ten. You can prove this by recognizing that you can come into a chain of trials at any point, even at the ninth trial, and recognize that your odds are still one-to-ten. **In other words, chance—like nature—has no power to do anything, since it has no being. Nothing cannot do something.**

Here lies the difference in the critical thinking of a scientist and an engineer. I have a degree in both and practice and teach both, and I understand very well that a scientist is free to imagine and explain anything, but it takes an engineer to make things work. Therefore, when a fantasy such as evolution is taught, I have to ask, *How can this strange theory actually work?*

LOCOMOTION

Many cells contain short hair-like outgrowths of the surface membrane called *cilia*. These are the method of locomotion allowing the cell to rotate or move forward or backward. Other cells have *flagella*, a long, thin tail that provides locomotion through a lashing movement. Many types of bacteria also have *flagella*. This designed method of microscopic locomotion using a motor-like mechanism is impossible for evolutionists to explain by random, closely bound, interdependent cellular masses.

A scientist could think, *A plant can't move from its location, except as seed, by exterior actions. An animal must move in order to differentiate it from plants. I see these cilia on the simplest animal organisms. How could these microscopic motor-like machines have evolved? Perhaps, given enough time, the association of organics—even DNA and RNA, amino acid, etc.—could cause some accidental improvement in the DNA to allow the appearance of cilia.* **On the other hand—an engineer would think—show me the chemical reaction that causes this evolution, and I'll not only believe it, I'll duplicate it and give humanity an unheard-of gift.**

SIGHT

Somewhere in the evolution from plants to animals or, as some believe, the branching from simple cells to plant or animal cells, animals *evolved* eyes and plants did not. The anatomy of an eye includes a very complex cornea, the iris for adjusting entering light, the pupil opening, the adjustable lens, and the retina, which receives the image. Then it really gets complicated when the image is transmitted to the brain as a memory.[5]

Two of the more difficult facts for an evolutionist to explain are the compound eyes of insects and the sensing of color. Among mammals, only primates see in color. On the other hand, some bony fishes, reptiles, birds, and bees do. The conclusion has to be that color vision is programmed and coded by a Creator and not evolved.[6]

Darwin in *The Origin of Species*, page 155, wrote this: "To suppose that the eye, with all its inimitable contrivances for adjusting the focus to different distances, for admitting different amounts of light, and for correction of spherical and chromatic aberration could have been formed by natural selection, seems, I freely confess, absurd in the highest possible degree."

Given this information, a scientist could say, *Wouldn't it be interesting if billions of contacts between organic molecules allowed the formation of a cornea, iris, lens, and retina that could electronically transmit the visual stimuli to the brain as a thought?*

An engineer would say, *If your theory is correct, show me the specific steps that occurred to form new DNA, so I can determine if the reaction has been* observed, documented, and repeated. *If it has, I can develop an eye biochemically.* **Also, did the different parts of the eye and brain evolve at different times and remain dormant until other parts had evolved so that sight was successful? Just show me the evidence, and I'll take it from there. Otherwise, sorry, but I don't believe you.**

Flight

The scientist: *At this point in the process of evolution, we have animals in the sea and on the land. Wouldn't it be nice if the land life could become more mobile through flight?*

The engineer: *Tell me how the bones started becoming lighter without weakening the structure of the species and preventing survival. Tell me how this potential flying animal decided it wanted feathers to control aerodynamics. Did one feather develop first—just the shape of a feather, like a scale? Tell me and I'll design a much more efficient airplane that is self-sustaining and gathers its own food for energy. But first I need to see the facts so that I won't waste my time with fantasy.* **And by the way, what is the decision force that designs the next step of evolution? Does chance have intelligence, does nature, or is it a higher spiritual power?**

Some evolutionists theorize that gliding preceded flying, but there is no evidence that gliding ability precedes flight ability, as demonstrated in flying fish and squirrels. Fossils of animal limbs have no relationship to bird-wing fossils. There is no evidence for the evolution of feathers, nor has there been a discovery of a scale-feather. There is no evidence of cold-blooded (reptile) to warm-blooded (bird) evolution.[7]

Genetics

The information presented in this section, unless otherwise referenced, is taken from work by Nathaniel T. Jeanson, PhD, and James J. S. Johnson, JD, ThD, from *Acts & Facts,* published by the Institute for Creation

Research, Dallas, Texas, in 2014 and 2015. Direct quotes are shown in quotation marks with dates of publication.

Charles Darwin knew nothing of genetics or DNA, which is the only real evidence of genealogical relationships. "Because DNA—not a fossil, anatomical structure, or geographical location—is transmitted at the moment of conception, only DNA directly records a species's genealogy" (February 2015). Now we have DNA sequencing information from thousands of species. There are three major lines of genetic evidence that supposedly supports evolution:

- Relative Genetic Similarities—"The hierarchical classification of life, based on anatomy and physiology" (September 2014). At conception, DNA is transmitted through both the sperm and the egg imperfectly. Each generation grows more genetically distant. This theory places the species with similar DNA in the same branches of Darwin's "tree of life" (i.e., man close to apes, farther from reptiles, and even farther from invertebrates like insects). But this categorization allies equally well to proving design.
- Absolute Genetic Differences (September 2014)—The comparison of the expected genetic imperfections in DNA transmission with time can predict differences and similarities. These calculations by evolutionists prove that their theory of predictable DNA change and their timetable of millions of years are radically flawed. For instance about 900,000,000 DNA letter differences exist between humans and chimpanzees, revealing a similarity of 70 percent. The similar DNA is understandable because of the two species' similar characteristics. There are also similar DNA sequences, on a lesser scale, between humans and reptiles and even plants. But according to evolutionary time scale, these human/chimpanzee differences **would have occurred in only six million years—a much shorter time than predicted. In**

The Future of Species

effect, the classical evolutionary time predictions are being destroyed rapidly as more accurate DNA mapping is developed.

* Junk DNA—"Since the mechanism of evolutionary change is based on genetic mistakes, evolutionists expect the genomes of certain species to be littered with useless (or junk) DNA" (September 2014). Indeed the very *engine* of evolutionary change is the genetic mistakes themselves, which allow for interspecies evolution. Recent research has shown that more and more of these "mistakes" or pseudogenes are functional, and there is not nearly as much junk DNA as predicted.

The coding in DNA *represents the opposite of chance. Randomness in any code sequence destroys the code...It is hugely paradoxical that some scientists suggest randomness could have given spontaneous birth to code sequences as super specific as those of the genetic code.*[8]

Recent DNA mapping shows radically different patterns of DNA in supposedly evolved species and has refuted Darwin's tree example that depicts evolutionary progress. **Similar strands of DNA are logically required to allow similar functions and characteristics, but they do not require a continual evolutionary progress. There is instead more evidence of a devolutionary movement.**

If chemicals combined by an electrical force—as many evolutionists claim—to form a compound that could duplicate itself and eventually become a living cell, that compound would have to be a molecule of DNA. In order for DNA to duplicate itself, there would have to be the presence of amino acids, sugar, and phosphate. As further electrical charges produced more DNA, the original molecule would be destroyed, since as a protein, DNA is very sensitive to heat and pH changes. DNA has been produced from a virus but never from an inorganic. A virus can only duplicate itself within a bacterium, plant, or animal cell, under normal conditions. A virus is therefore dependent upon higher levels of life for reproduction.[9]

Likewise, only the division of a DNA cell can produce DNA, where each original cell unwinds, and against each a new strand is built up, forming four strands, so that each new double strand of DNA consists of half-new and half-old DNA.[10]

1 Charles Darwin, *The Origin of Species* (New York, NY: Bantam, 1999) 400. 2 Carol Cleland, "Defining Life," *Astrobiology Magazine*, (June 19, 2002).
3 Dorothy Allford, MD, *Instant Creation—Not Evolution* (New York, NY: Stein and Day, 1978) 51.
4 Robert M. Hazen, *Genesis, The Scientific Quest for Life's Origins* (The National Academies Press, 2005).
5 Randy J. Guliuzza, "A Camera Made from Living Tissue!" *Acts & Facts* (July 2015).

6 Michael Pitman, *Adam and Evolution, A Scientific Critique of Neo-Darwinism* (Baker Book House, 1984) 216.
7 Ibid.215
8 Ibid, 53
9 Allford, *Instant Creation—Not Evolution*,51.
10 Pitman, *Adam and Evolution, A Scientific Critique of Neo-Darwinism*,53

CHAPTER 21

Chemical Changes, Living Animal Organic to Humans

Isn't all of philosophy like writing in honey? It looks wonderful at first sight, but when you look again it is all gone. Only the smear is left. Albert Einstein, 209

NOT SURPRISINGLY, DARWIN DOES NOT explain how animals evolved into humans; he just assumes they did. His leap of faith is the same as all post-Darwin evolutionists have made in their effort to be relevant. He resorted to philosophy instead of science, and his result was no more clear than a "smear of honey." Darwin inferred "from analogy that probably all the organic beings that have ever lived on this earth have descended from one primordial form, into which life was first breathed."[1] On the other hand, Einstein warned that "every reminiscence is colored by the way things are today, and therefore by a delusive point of view."[2]

Biology textbooks teach that animals evolved through Darwin's "Tree of Life" to the level that we call human. In most evolutionary thought, humans are just an evolved species of animals, and there is no need to explain it further. **But recent DNA testing and mapping have contradicted evolutionary predictions at levels that disprove Darwin's "Tree of Life."** Humans have about 3 billion DNA letters containing genes. Of these letters, about 900 million, or 30 percent are different between humans and chimpanzees.[3] Humans share more DNA with apes than they do with frogs or insects or vegetables, but that is reasonable in a designed world, since certain species function similarly in accordance with their similar DNA. Researchers have found that we share half of our DNA with bananas.[4]

The following are estimates of how much of our DNA is shared with various species in a current online article from *National Geographic*, intended to demonstrate the truth of evolution:

- Chimp: 90 percent
- Mouse: 88 percent
- Cow: 85 percent
- Dog: 84 percent
- Zebra Fish: 73 percent
- Platypus: 69 percent
- Chicken: 65 percent
- Fruit Fly: 47 percent
- Honey Bee: 44 percent
- Round Worm: 38 percent
- Wine grape: 24 percent
- Baker's yeast: 18 percent

Source: Javier Herrero, European Molecular Biology Laboratory

The latest DNA research is proving that these similarities in DNA between species are because of some of the basic functional similarities—such as life, vegetative or animal, land, water, or air dwelling, four or two legged—rather than an evolutionary relationship. As Einstein so deeply believed, we can advance our scientific knowledge only by the study and respect of God's Creation. **The most quickly advancing science today is the study of DNA, and these studies are exploding the entire theory of evolution with a big-bang level of energy!**

Dinosaurs Preceded Humans

Evolutionary theory consistently teaches that dinosaurs preceded humans in the evolutionary scale, and yet the Bible and other literature teaches otherwise:

- "And God made the beasts of the earth according to their kinds" (Genesis 1:25).
- "Behold, Behemoth, which I made as I made you; he eats grass like an ox. Behold, his strength in his loins, and his power in the muscles of his belly. He makes his tail stiff like a cedar; the sinews of his thighs are knit together. His bones are tubes of bronze, his limbs like bars of iron. He is the first of the works of God" (Job 40:15–19).
- Pliny the Elder referenced large dragons in his *Natural History*.
- *Fossil Legends of the First Americans*, written by A. Mayor in 2005 and published by Princeton University Press, lists stories of dinosaurs from Native American Indians.
- Many early European stories speak of dragons and other large monsters, which may or may not be fantasy.
- Biblical accounts of the early patriarchs recorded that they lived over nine hundred years, and reptiles—unlike humans—continue to grow all of their lives and would reach enormous sizes in old age.

Recent science has confirmed these biblical and secular accounts:

- **Material extracted from *Tyrannosaurus rex* and duck-billed hadrosaur bones, thought to be sixty-five million years old, contained soft tissue and proteins that should have degraded before fifty thousand years ago.[5]**
- Evolutionists believe that theropod flying dinosaurs are ancestors of feathered birds, but all supposed feathers have been determined to be either scales or of vegetative origin.[6]

The Missing Links

Evolutionists speak of the "missing links" that connect primates and humans, and school textbooks have accepted their conclusions without investigation. The following examples are of the more interesting claims:

- **Lucy**: Donald Johanson discovered Lucy in Africa in 1974, and the bones were estimated to be 3.17 million years old. **Since then most scientists have concluded that Lucy was an extinct gibbon, a type of ape.**[7] Recent CAT scans have shown conclusively that Lucy did not walk upright, as was theorized.[8][9]
- **Ida**: Ida was discovered in Germany in 1983 and was estimated to be 47 million years old. **Ida turned out to be a lemur.**[10]
- **Ardi**: Ardi was discovered in 1992 in Ethiopia and was estimated to be 4.4 million years old. **Ardi is now thought to be a form of monkey.**[11]
- **Neanderthal Man**: Bones were discovered in the middle 1800s in Germany's Neander Valley. **Genome research has shown that the Neanderthal Man was fully human, related to current Eurasians and interbred with modern humans.**[12]
- **Java Man**: Eugene Dubois discovered Java Man in 1891 and later admitted that Java Man was a giant gibbon.[13]
- **Piltdown Man**: Announced in 1912 and later discovered to be a fraud.[14]
- **Homo erectus**: These skeletal types have been shown to exist contemporaneous with those of modern humans and some of their features can be found among living populations.[15][16]

Dennis Petersen said, "It has been observed that taken all together, if you could gather all the fragments of skulls and other bones from all the so-called hominid relics found in the last century the sum total of them would not fill even one coffin."[17]

In summary, even though we have been indoctrinated with the illustrations showing the ascent of modern man from a monkey or ape, the fossil record does not support this evolutionary theory. It instead confirms the biblical account of a supernatural Creation by God.

---

1 Charles Darwin, *The Origin of Species* (New York, NY: Bantam Books, 1999) 395.
2 Alice Calaprice, *The New Quotable Einstein* (Princeton, NJ: Princeton University Press, 2005) 144.
3 Nathaniel T. Jeanson, "Darwin vs. Genetics," *Acts & Facts* (September 2014).
4 Henry M. Morris III, *Your Origins Matter* (Institutes for Creation Research, 2013) 25.
5 James J. S. Johnson, Jeffrey Tomkins, and Brian Thomas, "Dinosaur DNA Research," *Acts & Facts* (October 2009).
6 Frank Sherwin, "Did Dinosaurs have feathers?," *Acts & Facts* (August 2014).
7 Morris, *"Your Origins Matter"* 22.
8 Brian Thomas, "Lucy's New Foot Bone Is Actually Human," *Acts & Facts* (April 2011).
9 Brian Thomas, *Stones and Bones*, (Eight Mile Plains, Australia: Creation Ministries International, 1994) 13.
10 Morris, *Your Origins Matter.* 22
11 Ibid.
12 "Identifying Neanderthal Man," *Acts & Facts* (March 2011).
13 Dennis R. Petersen, *Unlocking the Mysteries of Creation* (Christian Equippers International, 1987) 118-123.
14 Ibid. 118-123.
15 Carl Wieland, *Stones and Bones* (Creation Ministries International, 1994) 13.
16 Peterson, *Unlocking the Mysteries of Creation* 118-123.
17 Ibid. 118-117.

Book 2
The Present

CHAPTER 22
Introduction

*I have never obtained any ethical values from
my scientific work. Albert Einstein, 19*

WE, AS HUMANS, COEXIST IN the twenty-first century with plants and animals in a restless state of uncertainty about our past and our future. We either believe that we have inherited an earth from nature or from God that is so fragile that we must save it from ourselves, or we believe that our earth is so stable that we can do anything we desire, and nature will have the resilience to survive. The purpose of Book 2 is to examine the state of our earth and its inhabitants as they currently exists, in order to predict our future.

Most evolutionists—especially evolutionary scientists—only address the environment as opposed to the intellectual, mental, ethical, and moral state of humans when they consider the future of species. This concern contrasts radically with the Creation view of Genesis, that God created the natural universe for human benefit and enjoyment and as a demonstration of God's omniscience and love.

In this section, the state of the environment will be addressed first, followed by the present state of its human inhabitants. My opinion pertaining to the present state of the environment is based on my experience as an environmental engineer. My opinion concerning the present state of the human part of the environment is based on my graduate-school education in microbiology, biochemistry, and epidemiology, my master's degree thesis work, which was done in the Vanderbilt Medical School, and my research since then. It is also based on my interpretation of scripture. Some may disagree with my conclusions, but if I have encouraged you to research and think about our present condition, I will have succeeded. **I would request only that you seek to rationally and prayerfully justify your position, scientifically, if there is a natural disagreement or, biblically, if there is a theological disagreement. Then God will reveal the truth!**

CHAPTER 23
The State of Inorganics and Organics

§

*I do not like to state an opinion on a matter unless
I know precise facts. Albert Einstein, 1943, 13*

INTRODUCTION

THIS CHAPTER WILL TAKE A side look at the chemistry of the present natural reality in order to present a small summary of the science of nature. The purpose is to allow the serious student or skeptic to understand nature—which is the environment—how it affects us today, and how it will affect us in the future.

INORGANICS

As explained previously, inorganics exist in the air, the water, and the soil—three realms of nature. Inorganics exist in the air in the form of noble nonreactive gases and reactive gases such as oxygen, nitrogen, and carbon dioxide, plus water vapor. Throughout history, these gases have remained consistent in their relative composition, except for carbon dioxide.

In bodies of water, inorganics exist as metallic or nonmetallic elements, molecules, salts, or compounds, which may change states to become gases or solids but exist permanently as elements.

In the soil, inorganics also exist in gases, liquids, or solids as elements, molecules, salts, or compounds and are subject to change of state and form. But again, mass/energy exists forever.

These three realms of nature support all organics.

In space, inorganic gases such as hydrogen, helium, argon, nitrogen, and even oxygen exist. Metals such as iron, aluminum, and magnesium exist, as well as nonmetals such as carbon and sodium, but no organics exist in space.

ORGANICS

The living animals on this earth depend on the air to breath oxygen, as an electron acceptor to metabolize organic food as their electron donor. In the process of metabolism, nutrients in solution in the form of hydrocarbons, nitrogen, phosphorous, and metallic micronutrients, through osmosis and catalyzed by enzymes, pass through bacterial cell membranes of animals and are converted into useful energy and carbon dioxide.[1]

Plants depend on sunlight and water to produce oxygen and glucose through photosynthesis.

Plants require the carbon dioxide produced by animals and glucose, and animals require the oxygen produced by plants and glucose, in order to have a balanced environment.[2] God created this **wonderfully balanced nature to operate in a self-sustaining manner, unduplicated in the universe. If any of these processes becomes even slightly out of balance, the entire living organic balance will be at risk.** This is the reason for pollution control.

The three realms of our natural environment receive unnatural organic and inorganic pollutants from the other realms as well as from the life or growth within the realms. These pollutants are transported from the realm in which they were created by natural processes or by human activities (which could be defined as natural activities just as well as animal activities), into a different realm or back into the same realm. These pollutants may be identical to their created form, or natural or human activities or processes may chemically altered them.

Air Pollution

From the beginning of civilization, cooking and heating have been the source of air pollution from burning animal-, vegetable-, and petroleum-based hydrocarbons—whether wood, peat, dung, fat, vegetable oil, animal oil, petroleum oil, natural gas, or coal. In the air, these hydrocarbons (organics), residual inorganic vapors (such as CO_2 and H_2S), and particulate pollutants receive no beneficial treatment, are not normally purified or broken down, but are only dispersed—except for absorption and transfer to the ground by rainwater. Also, inorganics such as NO, NO_2, and SO_2 can have thermal or photochemical reactions in the presence of oxygen and/or sunlight to form different compounds. There can also be reactions on the surface of particulates or in solution that cause some chemical changes.

Due to wind and thermal activity, this dispersion of pollutants in the air can be regional or international in scope. The dispersed pollutants can remain in the air permanently or at least for long periods of time, especially if they are vapors or gases. If the pollutants are lighter than air, or close enough to the specific gravity of air, they can rise, or wind and thermal currents can carry them higher in the atmosphere. If the pollutants are particulates, or heavier than air, they can settle or be carried by air movement back to the surface. Therefore air pollution may be dispersed in the air, or it may be carried to bodies of water or to the ground. The 1883 eruption of the Krakatoa volcano raised the average global temperature by as much as 2.2°F until 1888, according to Wikipedia, because the particulates formed caused a greenhouse effect as explained below.

Nature itself contributes to air pollution through vegetative and animal decay and through domestic and wild animals. **It has been estimated that domestic animals use 30 percent of the world's ice-free land, consume 8 percent of the world's fresh water, and produce 18 percent of the world's greenhouse gases, which is more than all forms of transportation.**[3] The following subsections, "Carbon Dioxide as a Pollutant," "Global Warming," and "Climate Change" present further information addressing the concern of how environmental changes could affect the future of species.

Carbon Dioxide as a Pollutant

In the atmosphere, carbon dioxide (CO_2) has varied in concentration from 318 parts per million(ppm) (0.0318 percent) in 1958, to 403.7 ppm in May of 2015.[4] Because of this unnatural increase, we should have an interest in preserving our air as it was originally created, or it could affect the delicate balance of our sensitive environment. Some of the information in this section is taken from *A Christian Environmentalist* by E. Roberts Alley.

Industrialization of our society has caused a continuing increase in the concentration of CO_2 in the atmosphere. The Environmental Protection Agency (EPA) has listed CO_2 as a greenhouse gas (GHG) that can contribute to the greenhouse effect by limiting back radiation of light coming to the earth. Many other GHGs have been eliminated or reduced by regulations, but CO_2 is the natural emission from animals breathing and the product of combustion, and as such it is much more difficult to control. According to *Carbon Sequestering*, the following sources and sinks (final storage locations) are annual estimates of the global CO_2 cycle during the 1990s:[5]

CO_2 Source	GtC*	CO_2 Sink	GtC*
Human and animal respiration	60.0	Vegetation (photosynthesis)	61.7
Deforestation	1.4	None	0
Fossil fuels	6.0	None	0
Decay of ocean vegetation	90.0	Ocean uptake	92.2
Source total	157.4	Sink total	153.9

* Billion metric tons of carbon from CO_2= gigatons carbon (GtC)

These estimates indicate that an estimated 3.5 GtC per year enters and remains in the atmosphere.

Recent research has attempted to quantify the loss and gain of CO_2 in the ocean due to temperature variation, but these estimates are difficult to substantiate because of the variability of ocean temperatures due to geography, seasons, and currents.

The ocean is estimated to contain about forty thousand GtC of CO_2.[6] If vegetative sequestration remains the same, the oceans would only increase CO_2 by 8.75 percent in one thousand years, but because of the logarithmic nature of pH, **there could be a gradual lowering of ocean pH caused by human activities (deforestation and fossil fuels), which could affect the growth of coral reefs and, consequently, a loss of local ocean biomass.**

The vegetation sink for CO_2 has a potential, through management policies, to affect the sequestration of human-caused CO_2 emissions. **Because of the increase in vegetative growth in the United States in recent years, there is a trend of net increase of CO_2 sequestered; but in the entire world in 2000, there has been a net annual reduction of CO_2 sequestration twenty times larger than the US increase.** [7]

The EPA has estimated that through changes in agricultural soil and forest management, tree planting, and biofuel substitution, the United States could increase its vegetative sequestration by 30 to 90 percent. In 2002, about 12 percent of the total CO2 emitted in the United States was sequestered.[8]

It should be emphasized that young forests use more CO_2 per acre than old forests. Young trees, like teenagers, metabolize more rapidly—using more CO_2—and old forests have more products of decay, which produce CO_2. **It has been estimated that a tree utilizes about 2.52 pounds of CO_2 per day.**[9] **This means that roughly one twenty-five-year-old tree is required to take up CO_2 exhaled by an average man, according to the "Carbon Dioxide" entry in Wikipedia.**

There is much discussion about nonfossil energy, especially solar power. This energy source is certainly attractive in rural areas instead of electric wiring, but the practicality of solar energy being a long-term solution is very limited. As an example, **the population of the United States is about 319,000,000 today, and the total solar panel area required to serve that population is greater than the land area of Delaware** (2,343 square miles versus 1,949 square miles). This ratio becomes much more critical in more populous countries.

A more practical solution than solar energy would be to require all industrial polluters emitting CO_2 to plant trees. Each year, industries could plant an equivalent number of trees, within a reasonable distance of the company's discharge, to take in the business's CO_2 emissions. It seems unreasonable to abandon an efficient source of energy (fossil fuel) with the hope of an impractical solution (solar power) without exploring carbon control by tree planting.

Global Warming

Since 1990 the United States has regulated the discharge of certain ozone-depleting chemicals such as Freon to prevent destruction of the ozone layer, which protects us from solar ultraviolet radiation and the potential of global warming through the greenhouse effect. Since the last few years of the twentieth century, even more concern has developed over the effect of greenhouse gas (GHG) emissions on global warming and global climate change, and many nations have organized to encourage international regulation of greenhouse gases.

The greenhouse gas effect theorizes that the ozone layer in the stratosphere (up to five to ten miles) collects GHGs, which allow solar radiation to pass through, but restricts its return to the mesosphere (up to thirty miles high), thereby increasing global temperatures, as in a greenhouse. By far the largest GHG is water vapor, representing around 90 percent of the greenhouse gas volume.[10]

In the 1970s the concern was for global cooling; in the 1980s and 1990s, that concern changed to global warming; and in 2009, when global temperatures plummeted, the concern changed again from global warming or cooling to climate change—in order to explain the effect of weather but not necessarily the cause of weather.

One theory is that regional warming, especially of certain areas of the ocean, can affect global climate, even if warming is not consistent. Much effort has been expended in relating cause and effect, and to date the most reliable relationships have been either GHGs or solar activity. Global temperature has been graphed with manmade carbon-dioxide emissions and carbon dioxide in the atmosphere. Both theories have had difficulty explaining radical variations in relationships from year to year, even though long-term emission trends are reasonably consistent. Carbon dioxide (CO_2) has been selected for further study, since it is considered the most likely manmade GHG candidate.

A second concern for manmade CO_2 emissions arises from the realization that CO_2 can be sequestered (absorbed or stored) in only three ways: vegetation, bodies of water, and soil. All nonsequestered CO_2 remains in the air.

All vegetation uses the sun's photosynthesis as an electron donor and CO_2 as an electron acceptor to produce energy and emit oxygen. All animal life uses food as an electron donor and oxygen as an electron acceptor to produce energy source and emit CO_2. Therefore, the more vegetation that exists in an area, the more CO_2 sequestering and the less CO_2 accumulation in the air, water, or land. Algae—an exception—act as a plant during the day, producing oxygen, and as an animal at night, producing CO_2.

The land is a relatively insignificant sequestering agent for CO2 since the bacteria in soil actually produce CO2, and most soil CO2 adsorption is actually absorption in the soil moisture.

The tendency for air to accumulate CO_2, as in most vapor/vapor mixing relationships, diminishes exponentially as the concentration in the air increases. This tendency drives more CO_2 to water surfaces. CO_2 in water forms carbonic acid, a weak acid that lowers the pH (the relative acidity) of the body of water. Lower water pH has been shown to negatively affect organic aquatic life, including coral reefs. It should be emphasized, though, that CO_2 is not the only killer of coral reefs. Large changes in water temperature can cause damage as well. Warm-water bleaching—and to an even greater extent, cold-water bleaching—have also been shown to severely damage two-hundred- to three-hundred-year-old coral in a span of five days.[11]

This is an example of why we shouldn't emotionally attack certain possible causes of environmental damage without researching available scientific resources and why engineering solutions—in

addition to scientific studies—should be presented to the public before panic sets in.

Adsorption of CO_2 into water vapor or droplets in the air also lowers the pH of rain and dew and makes them more acidic. This tendency is accelerated if sulfur dioxide (SO_2) is emitted into the air, forming sulfuric acid (H_2SO_4) or if oxides of nitrogen (NOx) are emitted, forming nitric acid (HNO_3) or if chlorine is emitted, forming hydrochloric acid (HCl). Coal-fired power plants, as well as other industrial sources, emit these strong acids, as well as CO_2, which causes acid rain. The author has completed extensive research documenting rainfall and dew at pH levels below 4, around one hundred miles downwind from major coal-fired power plants.

In the past decades, much effort has gone into global temperature predictions. The US National Oceanic and Atmospheric Administration reports global land and ocean temperatures from about 1880 to the present. Virtually all climate scientists accept these records that show a recovery from the Little Ice Age in the annual global temperature from 1880 to 1930, from about 59°F to 61°F; a warm period of 61–62°F between 1930 and 1950; a cooling at 61-59°F between 1950 and 1970; and an up-and-down variable—but gradual warming—from 1970 to the present, from 59 to 61°F. All temperatures are annual averages. **This NOAA data shows no significant global warming.**

Temperature extremes and temperatures in different geographical areas and ocean/land temperatures have varied much more during these periods. The difficulty in understanding global warming is not what has happened but why. Scientists have related temperatures to atmospheric carbon dioxide and to solar activity. CO_2 has had an exponential rise, as expected, since the industrial revolution, as more fossil fuel is used for energy. CO_2 has risen in a fairly smooth curve, but temperatures have been erratic with several periods of temperature drops while CO_2 is increasing.

A much closer correlation has been found when comparing global temperatures with solar activity. From 1860 to the present there is a close correlation as shown in *Environmental Effects of Increased Atmospheric Carbon Dioxide*, Journal of American Physicians and Surgeons (2007) 12, 79–90.

High solar activity is a combination of more solar flares, a strong solar wind, and more sunspots. The sun's electromagnetic field, under active conditions, envelops the earth and shields it from galactic cosmic radiation, producing fewer clouds and a warmer earth.[12]

It appears that we are currently in a long-term period of relatively mild global warming that is related more closely to solar activity than to any other variable, but the continued increase in human-caused CO_2 emissions must be considered as a factor that will tend to increase, and certainly not decrease, global warming.

As explained above, a more critical concern may be the gradual lowering of pH in oceans caused by CO_2 absorption.

Climate Change

Since global warming has been shown to be cyclical and more dependent on solar activity, recent concern has been centered on climate change. A summary of climate-related events costing more than one billion dollars from 1980–2012 is as follows (NOAA):

- Of the fifty-eight events from 1980–2003, 28 percent were hurricanes, 21 percent were nontropical floods, 17 percent were heat waves or droughts, and the rest of the categories were all under 10 percent.
- Of the sixty-three events listed since 2003, 22 percent were hurricanes, 11 percent were heat waves or droughts, and 44 percent were tornados.

Another interesting statistic from NOAA is the following list by decade of category hurricanes striking the mainland United States:

Decade	Cat. 5	Cat. 4	Cat. 3
1920s	0	2	3
1930s	1	1	6
1940s	0	1	9
1950s	0	3	6
1960s	1	1	4
1970s	0	0	4
1980s	0	1	3
1990s	1	0	4
2000s	0	1	6

Many of the more damaging hurricanes such as Sandy, Irene, Ike, and Katrina were lower categories, and the damage occurred mainly because of flood surge, length, or population density. It is virtually impossible to objectively relate these natural disasters to human-caused environmental conditions, since there is no consistency between the events and the amount of greenhouse gases, CO^2, or other pollution discharge. There is also no increase in the most damaging hurricanes over time.

It is probable that the earnest desire to relate human activity to environmental disasters is rooted in the need for many scientists to believe that we, as a human race, can affect and correct climate. The Bible teaches, and science confirms, that a supernatural, intelligent source created the climate and the weather, and we can protect ourselves from it but can do very little to change it.

WATER POLLUTION

Mankind has normally disposed of liquid wastes in the water or on the ground. The most common receptor has always been the water, since its usual movement is away from the source of pollution. Liquid, or even solid pollutants have historically resulted from eating, cooking, washing, feces, and urine. Where moving streams and rivers are found, civilization develops, and solid wastes such as trash, garbage, and feces have been dumped into these bodies of water for disposal. In the water some of the hydrocarbon portion of these pollutants can be broken down, by the oxygen present, into carbon dioxide and water, but most of the time, the bacteria and the oxygen in the water are insufficient to completely break down these hydrocarbons.

Due to the oxidation—along with water movement, tides, or waves—water pollution, even though somewhat diminished by natural treatment, is normally only local or regional in scope. But still, water can distribute organic pollutants.

Inorganic pollutants can remain in the water as widely distributed salts or dissolved chemicals, or they can float or settle in quiescent areas and collect as sediment in the bottom of streams, rivers, or the ocean. Volatile organics, which can evaporate at certain temperatures, and certain volatile inorganics, such as carbon monoxide and carbon dioxide, that are disposed of in bodies of water can return to the air.

During the same period that concern was developing over air pollution, the determination was made that water pollution was a health issue. This was due to the realization that many communicable diseases such as cholera, typhoid, salmonellosis, and amoebic dysentery are waterborne.

The first emphasis on discharges was to issue permits for direct discharges to a stream—whether from municipal, industrial, or private sources. These discharges typically enter a stream through one or more pipes or ditches. These sources were thought to include about 25 percent of the total water pollutants being discharged to US streams.

Later, indirect discharges—such as contaminated storm water carried in storm sewers or running in sheet flow over the ground—were issued permits for municipal, industrial, and private sources. These indirect sources were thought to include another 25 percent of total pollutants.

The remaining 50 percent of discharged pollutants were thought to come from agricultural and undeveloped areas. To date, the only agricultural, nonmanufacturing discharges typically regulated are animal feed lots.

The unregulated agricultural storm water discharges contain agricultural chemicals such as fertilizer (primarily nitrogen and phosphorous), herbicides, and pesticides. Undeveloped areas, fields, and forests discharge unregulated pollutants into streams and underground reservoirs, as by-products of vegetative and animal decay, animal wastes, and inorganic metals and nonmetals. **This last category of discharged water pollutants means that unregulated pollutants can be as high as 100 percent of the regulated pollutant load where the two coexist.**[13]

LAND POLLUTION

The third receptor of pollutants—the land—has, throughout history, been the only receptor of nonvapor/particulate pollution in arid areas, and certainly, along with water, is the primary receptor in all areas of civilization. Even today, the edges of growing urban areas are used for landfills and garbage dumps for the by-products of the inner development.

Excrement has historically been disposed of in latrines, privies, outhouses, or on the surface of the ground.

Of the three pollutant receptors, the soil provides the only significant biological means of pollutant treatment (water can provide some minor biological treatment), in the form of cellular oxidation, using bacteria that can convert organics primarily into carbon dioxide, water, hydrogen sulfide, nitrogen forms, and methane. Because of the relatively nonporous nature of soil, the result of soil pollution is normally local in concern—although in karst terrain, which is permeated with fissures and caves, pollutants can potentially be transported regionally, either underground or when they reach surface waters.

The disposal of solid wastes in the ground doesn't guarantee their treatment, especially if these solids are placed into cells, such as in a landfill, where they are not directly associated with the soil. Inorganics placed in the soil will normally remain as placed, which constitutes storage rather than treatment. I have excavated a fifty-year-old, abandoned landfill and have found readable newspapers and whole pieces of food.

As expressed above, land or soil and its vegetation are receptors of society's pollutant discharges. Vegetation, depending on its extent and its characteristics, can uptake liquids through transpiration, primarily through its roots. The pollutants in these liquids are either filtered out or absorbed or transpirated into the stems, branches, trunks, leaves, and blades. Some pollutants, such as nitrogen, phosphorous, and trace metals, act as nutrients to the vegetation. Carbon dioxide acts as an electron acceptor, but some pollutants are toxic to the plants or accumulate within them, making the plants toxic to animals and humans.

Pollutants that are not absorbed by vegetation may be adsorbed onto particles of soil, either from the air or from storm water or direct discharged flow. As explained above, bacteria in the soil can act to break down organic pollutants—ultimately into carbon dioxide and water. Bacteria have no effect on inorganic pollutants, other than in valence change or as anaerobic reducing agents affecting compounds like H_2S, NH_4, and PO_4. These inorganic pollutants can be considered to have "returned to the soil," although not necessarily in locations and concentrations at which they were initially removed from the soil.[14]

---

1 E. Roberts Alley, *Water Quality Control Handbook*, 2nd ed. (New York, NY: McGraw-Hill, 2007).
2 Wilbraham, Staley, Matta, Waterman, *Chemistry* (Boston, Mass.: Prentice Hall, 2005).
3 E. Roberts Alley, *A Christian Environmentalist* (USA: Xulon Press, 2013).
4 "Scripps CO2 Data—Mauna Loa Observatory," Scripps Institution of Oceanography, 2015, CO2Now.org., accessed October 30, 2014.
5 Lee Layton, online course based on the U.S. Department of Energy Report *Carbon Sequestration Research and Development* (Herndon, VA: PDH Center(1990).
6 Ibid.
7 *Trend Estimates of Land-Use Sequestration* (United States Environmental Protection Agency). Accessed October 17, 2012.
8 Ibid.
9 "Sequestration: How much CO_2 does a tree take up?" Tufts Climate Initiative, Accessed October 17, 2012.
10 Zeke Hausfather, *The Water Vapor Feedback, Yale Climate Connections* (Yale School of Forestry & Environmental Studies, 2008). Accessed November 4, 29012.
11 J. A. Kidney, J. M. Morrison, and V. B. Brinkhuis, "Coral Reefs," *Journal of the International Society for Reef Studies* (February 2012).
12 "Experimental Evidence for the Role of Ions in Particle Nucleation Under Atmospheric Conditions," *Proceedings from the Royal Society*, A.463 (2078): 385–396.
13 Alley, *A Christian Environmentalist*. 73
14 Ibid. 74

CHAPTER 24
The State of Humans, the Christian View

I am of the opinion that all the finer speculations in the realm of science spring from a deep religious feeling...I also believe that this kind of religiousness...Is the only creative religious activity of our time. Albert Einstein, 1930, 199

TO THOSE OF US WHO keep up with worldwide news, instead of just assuming what others say is the extent of what is happening, we must admit that, recently, good is decreasing and evil is increasing. This deadly trend started with Adam and Eve, and in the last century, it moved through Europe to the East Coast of the United States and later to the West Coast and is now threatening our heartland. For example, our governments allow us to murder live embryos, which science defines as humans (they have human DNA), for the convenience of the mother. Now the courts and governments favor one person (the one who has a choice) and grants this person more rights than another (who has no choice). An animal, and even a plant, that is less developed than an embryo has more rights in our world than an unborn human.

We allow, and even encourage, murder in the form of suicide—when, not only did God prohibit all forms of murder, suicide is obviously the most selfish act possible. All biblical references to suicide are negative. (See Matthew 27:3–8, Acts 1:18–19 (Judas); Judges 16:28–30, 1 Samuel 31:4–5, 1 Chronicles 10:4–6, 2 Samuel 17:23, 1 Kings 16:18, Amos 9:2, and Revelation 9:6.)

So murder is OK in our society, even though historically all civilized societies have prohibited murder—especially when murder is for the convenience of another (if the victim is too old, too undeveloped, or our personal enemy). We tend to pass our laws now to make us more comfortable and to reduce our anxieties, instead of for justice.

We educate our children with revisionist history, science, and art in order to teach them that everyone is alike, and no one should succeed though excellence to a higher level.

We allow our children to experiment with addictive substances and destroy their bodies and their minds.

We allow our children to be involved in social media and entertainment that presents sexual immorality as normal. We even educate them about sex with safe-sex procedures, rather than abstinence, through our how-to programs.

We let them live together and have sexual experiences before marriage since the media teaches us that is the norm, the fun, and the good. As a result, out-of-wedlock births are epidemic, and we sit by and complain instead of doing our part and risking the disapproval of our children. In the United States in 2013, 40.6 percent of births were to unwed mothers. Millennials—those born between the 1980s and the early 2000s—seem to have a malignant sense of entitlement and no tolerance for any delay of gratification.[1]

We encourage homosexuality, even as a justification for civil unions, and legalize secular marriage, when we do not give the same rights to other people who love each other and live with each other in a purer way, such as unmarried sisters, brothers, friends, or roommates. Our government seems to think that civil rights are synonymous with sexual activity. A civilized society would realize that love is not limited to sex.

To those who argue that things today are not worse than in the past, my answer would be, "Define 'the past' and define 'worse.'" There is no question that civilizations before Christ had worse and more abusive governments than with the United States today. My description of the deterioration of mankind is centered on the lack of morality as imposed by, or condoned, by governments. Christians can obviously define morality in different ways, but God does not. He has given us moral laws in the Old Testament and moral rules in the New Testament that make things clear to those who will listen and study with an open mind. These laws and rules supersede time. Only the sacrificial laws and some of the dietary and theocratic laws have been overruled—and those by specific directions in the Bible. List after list of what is moral and what is immoral, from God's perspective, is repeated in the Bible, starting with Genesis.

Beyond the numerous, but consistent, lists are biblical principles such as Jesus's Sermon on the Mount and the apostles' teachings. What Christian can deny that we are to be poor in spirit (in need of God's help), to mourn for God's forgiveness and healing, to be meek, to hunger and thirst for righteousness, to be merciful, to be pure in heart, to be peacemakers, and to be consistent when persecuted for righteousness and for Jesus's account (Matthew 5:3–12)? What Christian can disagree with Jesus's directions to fulfill the Old Testament law in ways that exceed the obedience of the scribes and Pharisees (Matthew 5:13–48)? **Who can say that we shouldn't protect our bodies and minds from drugs, tobacco, drunkenness, and sexual sin? Who can justify permanent bodily changes, decorations, and desecrations such as sex-change operations, tattoos, or cuttings? Yet evidence of these good principles is rare, and the bad things are *normal* in our society.** For some reason, the things that so obviously destroy God's temple, our bodies, are especially acceptable now, where they were socially shunned just fifty years ago. So the context of my concern is the recent deterioration of US society. People have always been—and will always be—bad, but I hope for a society that disapproves of biblical immorality, and we have developed just the opposite.

If our eyes are open to reality, we observe the following:

- Europe is not mostly Christian as it was in the past. In number of Christians, five of the top ten nations were European in 1970 and only one in 2010.[2]
- The nations with the largest populations of Christians today are countries like Mexico (95.9 percent), DR Congo (95 percent), Brazil (91 percent), and the Philippines (90.9 percent) where missionaries from Europe and the United States invested themselves years ago for Jesus—and these cultures were changed. In 2010 the United States was only 80.1 percent Christian—down from 90.9 percent in 1970.[3]
- Today there are more foreign missionaries to the United States than to any other country.[3] What does that tell us about our culture?
- We have become the police force of the world, forcing our questionable values on the rest of the world, and we are hated for this interference. It appears that we are not hated—as the media and the government would have us believe—for being Christian or being just but for being a bully.
- The United States is rapidly losing its Christian heritage and Christian values and is overtly following Europe in becoming an amoral, secular society.

How have we reached the present state of species? **I believe to a large extent that the Christian church has given up on the morality taught in the Bible, in a desperate attempt to be relevant and to attract more members—as if relevancy and membership is what Jesus taught, as opposed to renewed and changed lives**. We have compromised the truth of the Bible, including the Creation explanation, in order to become more attractive to *seekers*. We believe that it is preferable to get these curious people into our churches by entertainment, rather than the truth. Society in our world today is devolving morally, and the church is standing by wringing its hands and refusing to communicate the simple childlike solution to our dilemma: faith and belief in Jesus Christ and His Word.

We have become accustomed to thinking naturally, rather than spiritually, about our present and our future. We have accepted the evolutionary explanation that all facets of our existence—our bodies as well as our minds and characters—are inherited from lesser plants and animals that have no morals and can make no decisions, only react. To many, this is a comfortable belief. There is no blame, no responsibility, and no consequences outside of the ever-increasing rules to enforce equality of opportunity, intelligence, wealth, and physical prowess. **We tend to just medicalize bad behavior, thus eliminating any, or most, personal responsibility. In order for this utopian society to function, we must enforce tolerance of all beliefs and actions, since we conclude that they are not formed by choice but by evolutionary survival of the fittest.**

Interestingly, the belief in evolution is rather solid in the United States but (for reasons that are no doubt sociological but remain obscure) is less so in Europe.[4]

There have been periods in my lifetime when society has seemed to cease to grow in intellect, prosperity, and happiness. In the 1960s and '70s—when the cynicism and discontent of the beatniks was replaced by the defeatism of the hippies, who sought freedom from capitalism, sexual responsibility, and intellectualism, within the so-called peace of chemically enhanced escape—the moral culture of the country radically, and perhaps permanently, slowed down.

The results of this hippie mentality have been a lost generation of intellectualism and the resultant financial stagnation. Baby Boomers have raised children and grandchildren with the flexible morality they enjoyed in their immature years.

Around 2008 the United States opted for the security of government control as a solution to excessive private-business abuses in the industrial, health, and financial industries. Sadly, this appeal for personal peace and security has resulted in the loss of millions of jobs and hundreds of thousands of bankruptcies caused by overreaching government regulatory control. An exploding national debt and an imploding job market have again caused a generation of lost success, prosperity, education, and happiness.

The emergence in this century of libertarianism, as a serious counter to government control, has made the same lethal mistake as the hippies of the '60s and the Progressives of the 2000s, by contrasting individual freedom and responsibility with governmental protection and responsibility.

So what is the proper way to prevent our continuing lack of social, moral, and economic progress while continuing to enjoy peace and prosperity? I believe that all answers, especially to complex questions, are found in the scriptures. **You may ask why I tend to spiritualize everything. It is because life is spiritual, sin is spiritual, problems are spiritual, and answers are spiritual. There are no *natural* scientific answers to these questions.**

It appears that the Old Testament biblical model for government was a theocracy. That model would not work in the United States because of the failure of the Christian church to convince nonmembers of the truth of its convictions. But even if the United States were totally Christian, our Constitution and our commitment to freedom require the allowance of divergent beliefs, and that's a good and proper thing.

God didn't approve of having a warrior king for Israel—but one focused on keeping the Mosaic Law. The typical Old Testament model of government was to use the king and the priests to teach the truth of the scriptures, church lawyers for the interpretation of their constitution (the Bible), Levites to administer and manage the flock, and judges to enforce the rules of the Bible. Jesus, centuries later, was highly critical of the priests, lawyers, and judges for abusing their positions. Government seemed to be relatively unimportant to Jesus.

The Old Testament theocratic model of government is very similar to the model for the US Constitution. The legislative branch writes the laws to interpret and teach the requirements of the Constitution, the executive branch serves to implement the Constitution, and the judicial branch enforces the Constitution.

Today, as throughout history, the idea of individual freedom must be restricted in a society because of the interests and safety of other members. For instance, without a moral base, none of the Ten Commandments is rational. The four God-centered commandments make no sense, of course, without a God. The six societal commandments make no sense without a moral base. Our governments have made it clear that they are willing to murder unborn babies and let imperfect children and sick seniors die by destroying the health-care industry. Those in government wink at and practice adultery. They feel justified in stealing earned income from selected groups of the population in order to finance benefits and payoffs to other selected classes of voters. Politicians seem to feel that it is smart to lie, if the lie is just a means to an end. They teach the populace to covet the wealth of others and demand an unjust redistribution. Our leaders do not respect the Ten Commandments. **Some of us, in frustration and confusion, have promoted unrestricted freedom—short of a few untouchables, like murder and stealing—and favor unbridled freedom even in such social issues as prostitution, pornography, and drugs.**

The result of this over-reactive position of demanding legalization of these sins would cost society billions of dollars in crime, medical costs, and broken families. Unrestricted legal prostitution cannot be justified under the rule of the Ten Commandments because prostitution is sex outside of marriage. This irresponsible philosophy fails when we are forced to determine the minimum age of a legal prostitute. True individual freedom would allow prostitution at all ages; therefore, someone must judge the age of legality, thereby restricting true freedom arbitrarily. The societal health cost of legalized prostitution must be subsidized by the nonparticipating society. Likewise, pornography, under a truly free society, must be available to all ages.

The legalization of drugs—including tobacco, alcohol, and marijuana—has the same minimum age issue, but the most frightening result is the addictive nature of these drugs and the resultant medical cost, family destruction, and loss to the workforce. The societal costs of these addictions must, again, be borne by all—including the nonparticipating members—which is a form of theft.

The protection of society not only includes international protection but also internal protection from government theft, whether a person is rich or poor, to pay another person, whether they be needy or not. **Biblically, the care of the poor is voluntary, not an enforced responsibility. There is no fairness in the government, an industrialist, or a Robin Hood stealing from one person and giving to another.** Society's responsibility is to protect its citizens from thievery—especially if it is by the government and even if it is to pay for the addictions of the weak through prostitution, pornography, and drugs. That is the lethal weakness of the libertarians; they abuse the idea of liberty to the point that the weak and addicted are subsidized by the strong and responsible.

A true democracy has been said to be impractical since the easily manipulated, uneducated, and mentally disturbed members of society have equal voting rights as those more able to discern right and wrong. **But it is unfair to judge a person's right to representation by his educational or mental competence. So for a true democracy to function, there must be a way to prohibit unfair influence of society's members without limiting free speech.**

Socialist and communist states have been tried numerous times and have usually failed due to excesses and abuses of those in power. The adage "power corrupts, and absolute power corrupts absolutely" is true whether applied to governments, businesses, or churches. There are few proofs that bigness does not result in unfairness—whether to the governed, the consumers, the competition, or to church employees and members. A proof of this is to historically analyze the number of large governments, businesses, or churches that have survived over centuries without radical reorganization and/or name change.

Can a republic-type government prevent societal stagnation, such as the hippie movement, socialism, or libertarianism? Only if governmental power abuses are prevented, including those resulting from protest and liberty interests, which tend to unfairly redistribute power and wealth from those who have earned it (or inherited it, since we shouldn't prevent gifts) to those who have the vested interests.

Short of a theocracy, or a truly benevolent dictator (impossible because of original sin), the constitutional government of a republic is the only reasonable answer for fair government of a society. So we should praise God for what we have and work to make it better.

There are solutions that can start with us:

- We can prohibit our children from experimenting with addictive substances, so we will never have another lost age like the '60s and '70s, with millions of addicts begging for government subsidies at the expense of the more civilized people.
- We can fight to outlaw the recreational and nonprescriptive medicinal use of drugs and tobacco—not to reduce freedom but to protect our society and prevent the subsidy of the weak by the moral.
- We can turn the military into a legitimate police force to protect us from internal and external enemies, instead of an offensive force of national domination of the world.
- We can fight for laws allowing Christians in our nation to be free to pray and worship publically and have the faith to allow other religions to likewise pray and worship. God will prevail, not false gods.
- We can overturn Roe v Wade and assisted suicide so that no one has the right to murder.
- We can return the right to marry to churches, where it began.

The Bible teaches Christians that our present state is physical, just as we were created, but our spiritual state has fallen from the idyllic Garden of Eden existence when we walked with God, He provided for all of our needs, and we lived forever. That initial Creation was without death and without flaw in nature or in humans, and Adam and

Eve had the right of communicating directly with God, since they were created without sin and could therefore associate with a holy God. Adam and Eve's voluntary separation from God carried with it a curse on man to have pain and sweat in working for his sustenance, on women to have pain in childbirth—unlike most animals—and a curse on nature, including the entire universe, since it was all made for the benefit of humans. And the final curse is death. So, biblically, we exist today—and have existed since the Fall—in a cursed, and therefore flawed, environment that can destroy us and that we can theoretically destroy.

Summary

In the Christian view of our present state, there should be no real need to explain the ever-varying justifications for evolution; all is adequately explained in the Bible, and literally, no scientific evidence has been discovered that contradicts any of the biblical account. But in order to answer the normal evolutionary teachings of this generation, we will discuss various claims that are made with the expressed, or hidden, purpose of refuting God's Word.

---

1 Arch Warren, *Jesus: Light and Truth* (Nashville: Covenant Presbyterian Church, 2015).
2 *Christianity in its Global Context, 1970–2020* (Center for the Study of Global Christianity, Gordon-Conwell Theological Seminary, 2013) 15.
3 Ibid. 15
4 Alvin Plantinga, *Evolution, Neutrality, and Antecedent Probability: a Reply to Van Till and McMullen* (University of Notre Dame, Calvin Virtual Library of Christian Philosophy, 1991) 41 of 45.

CHAPTER 25

The State of Humans, the Secular View

If my theory of relativity is proven successful, Germany will claim me as a German and France will declare that I am a citizen of the world. Should my theory prove untrue, France will say that I am a German and Germany will declare that I am a Jew. Albert Einstein, 1922, 8

THE STATE OF OUR SOCIETY

THE SECULAR VIEW OF OUR present state and our origin is not based on a document or series of documents but is an ever-evolving fantasy of imagination and speculation, daily changing to explain that there is no god, or if there is He has started something and left it alone to fail or survive dependent on the power and intelligence of humans.

Since evolution teaches that our present state just evolved by chance, there is no need, under this philosophy or religion, to be concerned with the devolution of civilization or society. It happened, and we humans—as the secular gods of the earth—have a responsibility to make all humans and all animals healthy, happy, and comfortable. The logical humanist religion is that all animals and all humans must be equally treated, respected, and cared for to meet these needs. There is no place in this utopian view of society for differentiation between the inhabitants of the earth—due to inheritance, ambition, or physical prowess—other than with the managers or governors of the society, who must be treated differently in order to be able to effectively manage the rest of the world.

This sounds strange to say, but is the logical extent of evolutionary thinking. No one and no animal can be held responsible for its inherited actions. Morality is irrelevant. If the unfit do not survive, they are not supposed to, but as long as they do live, they must be equal in all ways to all others—just as are vegetables and animals, since they had nothing to do with their present situation. Equality rules, rather than fairness and justice.

The secular view of the human condition is that our heritage, our family, and our nation define us. There is some truth in that because those things form our experiences. But the truth is that God defines us. We are placed in a family and a country, but that is only a circumstance that does not completely define us.

The obvious result of this religion of humanism is chaos and corruption, as we are beginning to experience in our society today.

CHAPTER 26
Finding Myself

My life is a simple thing that would interest no one. It is a known fact that I was born, and that is all that is necessary. Albert Einstein, 1935, 12

THESE DAYS MANY YOUNG PEOPLE spend years trying to *find themselves* in order to understand why they are here in society and what they should do about it. Some feel that their true self will be found through overseas travel, some by drug experimentation, some by self-help gurus, and some by meditation. One self-help course asks these questions:

- Who am I?
- Where did I come from?
- What am I here for?
- How do I do it?
- Where am I going?[1]

Not coincidentally, these are the same questions we all ask, the same questions this book attempts to answer, and the same questions the Bible definitely answers. **Wouldn't it be nice if people would just immerse themselves in the Bible and save all of the money and time of self-help, while really and permanently finding themselves?** God made us the way we are, unique and special. We came from God's design for the purpose of praising Him and enjoying Him forever. We do this by believing in Him so that we can read His Word and understand His plan for us, and if we do this, we will spend eternity with Him in heaven.

---

1 "How to Find Yourself," Adrienne, July 27, 2015, http://www.experiencelifefully.com.

CHAPTER 27
Reinventing Myself

§

Why is it that nobody understands me, yet everybody likes me? Albert Einstein, 1944, 13

IF, WHEN WE THINK THAT we have found ourselves, we are not satisfied, our tendency may be to insist that we change—to reinvent ourselves. Many of us consider ourselves strong enough and smart enough to reinvent ourselves as a means of finding ourselves. That will be a frustrating journey because I cannot reinvent that which God has invented to His satisfaction. Reinventing basically means to leave your present personality, values, gifts, abilities—everything that God has given you—and take on the characteristics of someone else you admire or invent.

Melissa Kirk, of *Tiny Buddha*, states that she attempts "to go with the flow and roll with the punches as much as possible." That sounds good, as does most of the "Finding Myself" advice, but life without God will always be empty. We can deny the supernatural and attempt to find ourselves or reinvent ourselves, but no natural effort can change the will of God. We can feel better temporarily, but we can receive no long-term peace without becoming one with Christ (see chapter 31). **The long-term values of** *love, joy, peace, patience, kindness, goodness, faithfulness, gentleness, and self-control* **are the fruit of the Spirit and are, therefore, supernatural. (See Galatians 6:22.)** These values are available from the Holy

Spirit, God Himself, and all the self-help in the world cannot be as satisfying or complete.

We can attempt to find ourselves—or even reinvent ourselves—but without God our sin nature will prevail, and we will be back into our old selves before we pay the bill for our seminar.

CHAPTER 28
The Solution for our Present State

*It is people who make me seasick—not the sea. But
I am afraid that science has yet to find a solution
for this ailment. Albert Einstein, 1930, 114*

As God promised in Genesis 3, He has provided a solution to the curse and the resulting Fall of nature. Being a just God, He could not allow a sinful person to communicate with Him or to completely understand His plan for us to be one with Him, worship Him, and enjoy Him forever. God, being supernatural, is by definition holy—or set apart from—His natural Creation. Any contact with a sinful person would be impossible because of that holiness, but in His love, grace, and justice, He allowed Jesus (as Himself, Who lived the only sinless life in history) to be sacrificed in blood, in permanent payment (restitution) for the sins of the whole world. (See John 3:16–18 and Romans 3:26.)

What love! What forgiveness for us, who have always wanted to be God. If Adam and Eve hadn't sinned by wanting to be God, we would have. But even with this natural tendency that we have, God made no mistake when He said that His Creation was *very good*. He has blessed us with the ability to choose, and we have abused it, but still He has invited us home to His feast.

So our ultimate future is resolved—as we will discuss in "Book 3, The Future." But for now, we must exercise our dominion over His Creation as stewards and preserve what He created as *very good* until He replaces it.

In order to have the wisdom and power to accomplish this dominion, we must seek God's supernatural help. As we have discussed, that help is available. Jesus left the Holy Spirit, also called the Comforter and the Helper, in His place. John 14:26 says that the Holy Spirit "will teach you all things and bring to your remembrance all that I have said to you."

CHAPTER 29
The Re-Creation of the New World

§

The true value of a human being is determined primarily by the measure and the sense in which he has attained liberation from himself. Albert Einstein, 1932, 115

THE NEED FOR A NEW WORLD

WE HAVE SEEN SO FAR in "Book 2" that man has a biblical responsibility to protect and improve his environment but that—because of the fall of man, resulting in the curse of God and the decay of the environment—the complete recovery is impossible without the intervention of our Creator.

Some information in this chapter is taken from *A Christian Environmentalist*, by E. Roberts Alley, published by Xulon Press in 2013.

Romans 8:20–22 tells us the following: "For the creation was subjected to futility, not willingly, but because of Him who subjected it, in hope that the creation itself will be set free from its bondage to corruption and obtain the freedom of the glory of the children of God. For we know that the whole creation has been groaning together in the pains of childbirth until now."

So the Bible tells us that God sees forward to a time when nature is set free from the results of human sin so that it will no longer be caught in the pains of childbirth and will allow the final freedom of the children of God. The *decay* in verse 21 above is a description of our scientific law of entropy: "the degradation of the matter and the energy in the universe to an ultimate state of inert uniformity."[1] Entropy is one of the basic scientific arguments against evolution.

We must ask why the environment is in such a position that it has to be destroyed and replaced. As we have seen previously in Genesis 1 and 2, the environment was created good. Satan tempted Eve and Adam to eat vegetation (from the tree of the knowledge of good and evil), which they did since it was

- Good for food
- A delight to the eyes
- Desirable to make them wise

These words from Genesis 3:6 make it clear that Adam and Eve were tempted by the same tempter who tempts us today. And they were tempted to commit the same three basic sins, as expressed in Exodus 20:3–17 in the Ten Commandments, that we commit today:

- Greed (Commandments 5, 6, 7 and 8)
- Lust (Commandments 9 and 10)
- God envy (Commandments 1, 2, 3 and 4)

All of this started as a lie from Satan: "But the serpent said to the woman, 'You will not surely die. For God knows that when you eat of it your eyes will be opened, and you will be like God, knowing good and evil'" (Genesis 3:4–5). And it resulted in Eve and Adam lying to themselves: "So when the woman saw that the tree was good for food, and that it was a delight to the eyes, and that the tree was to be desired to make one wise, she took of its fruit and ate, and she also gave some to her husband who was with her, and he ate" (Genesis 3:6). This sin of wanting to be God was so grievous to God, that He did not even finish the sentence in Genesis 3, verse 22: "Then the Lord God said, 'Behold, the man has become like one of Us in knowing good and evil. Now, lest he reach out his hand and take also of the tree of life and eat, and live forever—." For man to live forever in a sinful condition was an unbearable thought, and God would waste no time to prevent it, so He sent Adam and Eve out of the Garden. Instead of man performing his priestly duty to guard and care for the garden, he was removed outside to work the ground. The priestly duty reverted to the cherubim and a flaming sword to guard the garden and the tree of life (Genesis 3:24).

All humans are tempted to sin for something that satisfies our greedy wants, that appeals to our lusts, or that gives us the knowledge of good and evil. These temptations are still, and always will be, our failing—especially the temptation to be God, which is the root of all evil. The difference between Adam and Eve originally, and fallen humans today, is that Adam and Eve had the ability to avoid sin, while we do not.

Without the grace of God, the payment of Jesus, and the power of the Holy Spirit, we are completely inadequate to resist these temptations. The Word of God in the Bible and the presence of His Spirit within us guard us from our temptation to want to be God. Ephesians 6:17–18a says, "and take the helmet of salvation, and the sword of the Spirit, which is the Word of God, praying at all times in the Spirit, with all prayer and supplication." See also Hebrews 4:12.

As a result of our ancestors' sins, God cursed the serpent: "cursed are you above all livestock and above all beasts of the field" (Genesis 3:14b). He gave the woman pain in childbirth and a position of submission to the man: "To the woman He said, 'I will surely multiply your pain in childbearing; in pain you shall bring forth children. Your desire shall be for your husband, and he shall rule over you'" (Genesis 3:16). He cursed the ground because of Adam: "And to Adam He said, 'Because you have listened to the voice of your wife and have eaten of the tree of which I commanded you, 'you shall not eat of it;' cursed is the ground because of you; in pain you shall eat of it all the days of your life'" (Genesis 3:17) and also Genesis 5:25. God required that Adam toil for his food and introduced sweat and death: "By the sweat of your face you shall eat bread, till you return to the ground" (Genesis 3:19).

He returned us to dust, and death came into the world for the first time (Genesis 2:17, 3:19, 1 Corinthians 15:21, 22, Romans 5:12, 15–17). *Sweat* is mentioned in the Bible only two other times, as a curse that God's servants had to be separated from: in Ezekiel 44:18 and in Jude 23. It is also mentioned in Luke 22:44, the passage about Jesus's agony in prayer before his crucifixion in the garden of Gethsemane, when His *sweat* became like drops of blood. Jesus's blood substituted for the curse in the Garden, but the result of the curse remains in the old world until the new heavens and earth are formed.

Romans 8:20–21 tells us that the creation longs and waits for the revealing of the sons of God: "For the creation was subjected to futility, not willingly, but because of Him Who subjected it, in hope that the creation itself will be set free from its bondage to corruption and obtain the freedom of the glory of the children of God."

Therefore, the effects of the Fall are as follows:

- Man against God
- Man against man
- Man against nature
- Nature against man
- Man against himself

When we are set free from the curse in the new world, our relation to the new environment in heaven is described to some extent in the Bible.

In the next part of this book, we will explore what may be our only hope for the survival of species in the near future—and what is definitely the only hope for our ultimate survival.

---

1 *Webster's Ninth New Collegiate Dictionary*, (Spingfield, Mass.: Merriam-Webster), 1990

Book 3
The Future

Part 1
The Future through God

CHAPTER 30
Introduction

The ancients knew something that we seem to have forgotten: that all means are but a blunt instrument if they do not have a living spirit behind them. Albert Einstein, 1939, 117

I BELIEVE THAT OUR ONLY hope for surviving as a species rests not in ourselves but in our Creator God. He designed us, provided an earth and a universe to sustain us, and taught us how to survive in His Creation. It appears that we have brought our art and our science to a screeching halt because we will not accept the fact that God created a beautiful universe to demonstrate good art and to demonstrate the mathematical order of all of His creation. Part of God's common grace to His fallen creation is that He permits man to discover more and more about His Creation through art and science.

Our society has ripped us away from the God of the Bible and fabricated a complacent, tolerant, and all-accepting god never envisioned before. This new god encourages us to feel good about ourselves, regardless of the hate and selfishness inside.

This god encourages our artists to use infidelity, sex, and strange families to redefine normal. This god encourages our scientists to practice experimental science, not for the purpose of developing new scientific laws, but to influence us to redefine fantasy as science.

In the United States, we are unable to be as close to God as we once were because of the pressure to conform to the world. We have allowed this devolving world to nibble away at our oneness with God to the point that we are farther from spiritual truth than before. Long-term world history seems to be a cycle of fall, rebellion, and renewal, differing in various countries. But here, at this time in history in the United States, we find ourselves in the fall and rebellion stages.

What is the answer to this spiritual, and even secular, devolution? We must admit that our basic intelligence is deteriorating through entropy and make up for that loss by submitting ourselves to the Holy Trinity so that we today can be just as one with God as were the apostles. Spiritual truth, including our spiritual maturity, *does not devolve*.

The law of entropy is limited to natural reality. Spiritual reality has no such limitations. It is the same today as it was throughout history because it is from God and not nature, and was not cursed.

Through the Holy Spirit, we can understand God's will as expressed in the scriptures, and we can be one with God because we have the same Holy Spirit. The Holy Spirit, as God, is truth. Therefore, we can know the truth today just as well as anyone ever could. And that includes the truth of art and the truth of science.

Our limitation, as we move into the future, is that we refuse to acquire truth and wisdom from the Bible through the Holy Spirit. It is our attempt to use our natural intellect to understand and communicate those truths. In order to reach the full potential for which God has created us, we must further submit ourselves to God, and we must more deeply and diligently study the scriptures with prayer. Only then can we be creatures of the future, truly ready for the return of Jesus and completely able to communicate those eternal spiritual truths to others.

In other words, the future of species is dependent not on science, but on oneness with God. Science can give us food, clothing, shelter, wealth, and entertainment, but those things are simply existence. Only reconciliation and oneness with God can give us truth, peace, and joy that will be lasting and everlasting.

No one, outside of God, can know the future. My opinion of the future of species is based on my extrapolation of the past and the present and my interpretation of the scripture. Some may disagree with my conclusions, but the goal of this book is to encourage the prayerful and thoughtful research and study that will reveal God's truth for the future of species and how we can do our part to prepare for it.

CHAPTER 31

Oneness with God

〉

In order to be a perfect member of a flock of sheep, one has to be, foremost, a sheep. Albert Einstein, 1954, 120

JOHN, THE DISCIPLE WHOM JESUS loved (John 13:23, 19:26, 20:2, 21:7, 20), spoke much of becoming one with God.

> I do not ask for these only, but also for those who will believe in Me through their word, that they may all be one, just as You, Father, are in Me, and I in You, that they also may be in Us, so that the world may believe that You have sent Me. The glory that You have given Me I have given to them, that they may be one even as We are one, I in them and You in Me, that they may become perfectly one, so that the world may know that You sent Me and loved them even as You loved Me (John 17:20–23).

Since God is Spirit, and we are natural, we might wonder how we can be one with the supernatural. Is that just another fuzzy Christian term used to impress others, or is it a real possibility? True, it is a spiritual step and not a natural one, but God wouldn't have written that instruction to us unless it was very real and practical.

Other verses further explain the mystery of being one with God and Jesus. 1 John 2:5–6 says, "But whoever keeps His Word, in him truly the love of God is perfected. By this we know that we are in Him: whoever says he abides in Him ought to walk in the same way in which He walked." 1 John 4:12 and 17 say, "No one has ever seen God; If we love one another, God abides in us and His love is perfected in us…By this is love perfected with us, so that we may have confidence for the day of judgment, because as He is so also are we in this world."

Paul also speaks of this critical relationship with God in 1 Corinthians 6:17: "But he who is joined to the Lord becomes one spirit with Him" and in Philippians 2:13: "For it is God Who works in you, both to will and to work for His good pleasure."

So we really can be one with God because, if we are Christians, we have been born again out of the death of our sin nature and into a supernatural life. **When Jesus left the Holy Spirit in His place, He left Himself, He left God, and He made us body and spirit because the Holy Spirit now indwells us—just as It did in Jesus as man. Oneness with God is not some vague thing He puts into me, it is actually God in me.**

The Holy Spirit can allow us to understand the "hidden wisdom of God" (1 Corinthians 2:7) and the "things freely given us by God" in His Word (1 Corinthians 2:12). The Bible teaches that when Jesus Christ saves us through regeneration, we are filled with the Holy Spirit. Jesus left the Holy Spirit as part of the Trinity with us in His stead. Consider these verses: "And behold, I am sending the promise of my Father upon you. But stay in the city until you are clothed with power from on high" (Luke 24:49). "And when He had said this, He breathed on them and said to them, 'Receive the Holy Spirit' (John 20:22). "And they were all filled with the Holy Spirit" (Acts 2:4).

As a result of regeneration, we can acknowledge that we have no real power or understanding without God, and we will receive the gift of the Holy Spirit, just like the apostles and disciples. When we receive that gift, we are regenerated as God's children with the inheritance of the disposition—or life—that was in Jesus, according to these verses: "In Him was life, and the life was the light of men" (John 1:4); "Again Jesus spoke to them, saying, 'I am the light of the world. Whoever follows Me will not walk in darkness, but will have the light of life'" (John 8:12); "I have come into the world as light, so that whoever believes in Me may not remain in darkness" (John 12:46).

We receive that gift of the Holy Spirit through belief and faith: "For everyone who has been born of God overcomes the world. And this is the victory that has overcome the world—our faith. Who is it that overcomes the world except the one who believes that Jesus is the Son of God?" (1 John 5:4–5).

And that belief must be like that of a child: "'Truly, I say to you, unless you turn and become like children, you will never enter the kingdom of heaven'" (Matthew 18:3). (See also Mark 10:15 and Luke 18:17.) We are taught to put away childish things but not childlike faith.

That life that Jesus puts into us through the Holy Spirit when we are saved enables us to discern between the natural and the supernatural and to more clearly see the revealed mysteries of God through Bible study and prayer. Prayer is how the life of God in us, through the Holy Spirit, is nourished.

These mysteries will only become completely clear in heaven, but our understanding in this life is sufficient for His purposes. Indeed, in heaven we will no longer have a need to understand; we will finally only be interested in God and His relation to us. Imagine how peaceful we will be then! 1 Corinthians 13:12 says, "For now we see in a mirror dimly, but then face to face. Now I know in part; then I shall know fully, even as I have been fully known."

CHAPTER 32

The New Heaven and New Earth

The most beautiful thing we can experience is the mysterious. It is the fundamental emotion that stands at the cradle of true art and true science. He who does not know it and can no longer wonder, no longer feel amazement, is as good as dead, a snuffed-out candle. It was the experience of mystery...that engendered religion. A knowledge of the existence of something we cannot penetrate, our perceptions of the profoundest reason and most radiant beauty, which only in their most primitive forms are accessible to our minds—it is this knowledge and this emotion that constitute true religiosity; in this sense, and in this alone, I am a deeply religious man. Albert Einstein, 1930, 199

GOD IN HIS GRACE HAS elected to tell us certain things about what Heaven will be like through His Word from Jesus, through prophets, through John's visions, and through parables.

Some of the information in this chapter is from *A Christian Environmentalist* by E. Roberts Alley and published by Xulon Press in 2013. Hebrews 12:25–29 contains a warning and prophesy:

> See that you do not refuse Him Who is speaking. For if they did not escape when they refused Him who warned them on earth, much less will we escape if we reject Him Who warns from heaven. At that time His voice shook the earth, but now He has promised,

"Yet once more I will shake not only the earth but also the heavens." This phrase, "Yet once more," indicates the removal of things that are shaken—that is, things that have been made—in order that the things that cannot be shaken may remain. Therefore let us be grateful for receiving a kingdom that cannot be shaken, and thus let us offer to God acceptable worship, with reverence and awe, for our God is a consuming fire.

These verses compare the shaking at Mount Sinai (Hebrews 12:18–21) with another shaking of the earth and the heavens as we come to Mount Zion (Hebrews 12:22–24). This future shaking will have the result of separating nature (the things that have been made) from the spiritual things that cannot be shaken.

In heaven we will finally dwell with God (Revelation 21:3). As His people, we will enjoy heaven's radiance—the beauty of inorganics in heaven: "like a most rare jewel, like a jasper, clear as crystal" (Revelation 21:11). (See also Revelation 21:18–21.)

Other inorganics that we use and enjoy today will survive in Heaven. We have seen that the inorganic creation of *water* from Genesis 1:1–7 survives as the river of the water of life in Revelation 22:1–2—flowing clear as crystal from the throne of God and of the Lamb. Jesus promised this in John 4:10–14, 7:38–39, and Isaiah 44:3.

Revelation 21:1b says that the "first heaven and the first earth had passed away, and the sea was no more." This promise may refer to earthly rebellion, chaos, and danger (the sea of the beast of Revelation 13:1, which will no longer be present). But it could mean that there literally will be no sea. Revelation 22:1–2 speaks of the river of the water of life flowing through the middle of the street of the city—the fresh water of the new heaven.

The inorganic creation of *minerals* from Genesis 1:2 survives as minerals, precious, and semiprecious jewels. The twelve jewels adorning the city's apostolic foundations, in Revelation 21: 19–20, correspond to the twelve Israeli tribe symbols on the breastplates of the high priest described in Exodus 28:17–20. These stones are also similar to those that Ezekiel described in Ezekiel 28:12–19 as having been in the Garden of Eden. These stones anointed the fallen angel Satan, and God will use them as a permanent reminder in heaven of the futility of the corruption of evil, and He will reclaim their beauty for His children.

Vegetation, created as described in Genesis 1:11–12, survives as new fruit trees (Revelation 22:1–2). God's perfect light and "the river of the water of life" will allow vegetation in heaven, just as it did in Genesis 1:2. We can read about this in Revelation 22:2: "through the middle of the street of the city; also on either side of the river, the tree of life with its twelve kinds of fruit, yielding its fruit each month."

So we will enjoy the beauty of organic plants, along with the beauty of inorganic gems. Interestingly, Revelation 22 verse 2b says that: "The leaves of the tree were for the healing of the nations," presumably because of the destruction of death. Vegetation, which originally provided sustenance for humans and animals, will, in the New Heaven, be used for the sustenance of the nations.

Animals survive as seen below as new wolves, lambs, lions, oxen, leopards, kids, calves, cows, bears, cobras, and vipers. Both wild and domestic animals are mentioned, but all are tame and in harmony with the rest of nature without the death of any of God's creation.

In Isaiah 65:25, we find that "the wolf and the lamb shall graze together; the lion shall eat straw like the ox." And in Isaiah 11:6–8, God tells us the following:

> The wolf shall dwell with the lamb, and the leopard shall lie down with the young goat, and the calf and the lion and the fattened calf together [or will feed together]; and a little child shall lead them. The cow and the bear shall graze; their young shall lie down together; and the lion shall eat straw like the ox. The nursing child shall play over the hole of the cobra, and the weaned child shall put his hand on the adder's den.

These verses make it clear that the curse at the Fall will vbe removed in the new Heaven. Some commentators interpret these words as referring to predatory nations, some to the millinial period prior to the new Heaven, and some alegorically or literally to heaven itself.

In the context of the entire Bible, humans survive, presumably, as same-age adults so that everyone is equal in heaven (Matthew 22:30, Mark 12:25). Compared to marriage, God is able to establish relationships of even deeper friendship, joy, and love in Heaven.

This new heaven and earth will not only give us a pure relationship to the nonhuman part of our environment but also to ourselves and other souls in heaven. The coexistence of domestic animals and humans with dangerous wild animals describes a heaven where the curse of Genesis 3 will be removed, and death, sickness, and sweat will not exist.

The old organics—vegetables, animals, and humans—that have died return to dust through death so that they do not survive as organics. Instead, God transforms them, through Jesus's blood, into a new life as new organics and souls in the new heaven and new earth.

In the new heaven and the new earth, the sun and the moon do not survive; there is no reason for them (Genesis 1: 14–18). God said that the purpose of the astronomical existence was to

- Separate day and night (Genesis 1:14)
- Act as signs (1:14)
- For seasons (1:14)
- For days and years (1:14)
- To give light (1:15)
- To govern the day and night (1:16)

But God replaces these purposes in Revelation 21 and 22.

Revelation 21:23 says, "And the city has no need for sun or moon to shine on it, for the glory of God gives it light, and its lamp is the Lamb." Isaiah 60:19–20 also prophesizes this, as does Revelation 22:5.

Since the sun and moon were created on the same day as the stars, it is logical to assume that there will be no stars in heaven. There will be no need for seasons, days, and years, since there will be no time. There will be no need for God to demonstrate His infiniteness, power, and wisdom; those characteristics will be obvious.

There will be no temple, "for its temple is the Lord God the Almighty and the Lamb" (Revelation 21:22). Isaiah 65:17 says, "For behold, I create new heavens and a new earth, and the former things shall not be remembered or come to mind." (See also Isaiah 66:22.)

Job 33:23–28 tells us that because Jesus ransomed us, our soul will be delivered from the pit in righteousness and our flesh will become fresh with youth and we will return to our days of youthful vigor.

2 Peter 3:13 says, "But according to His promise we are waiting for new heavens and a new earth in which righteousness dwells."

Revelation 22:14 says that we will have the right to the tree of life, which was present in the Garden of Eden along with the tree of the knowledge of good and evil of Genesis 2:17 and 3:22. No longer will the knowledge of good and evil be kept from us, and we will live forever.

Isaiah 25:8 tells us that "He will swallow up death forever; and the Lord God will wipe away tears from all faces, and the reproach of His people He will take away from all the earth, for the Lord has spoken." Paul quotes part of this verse in 1 Corinthians 15:54 and follows it in verse 57, which says, "But thanks be to God, Who gives us the victory through our Lord Jesus Christ."

1 Corinthians 15:26 says, "The last enemy to be destroyed is death." Revelation 21:4 says, "He will wipe away every tear from their eyes, and death shall be no more, neither shall there be mourning, nor crying, nor pain anymore, for the former things have passed away." Jesus's death and resurrection have defeated death. As 1 Corinthians 15:44 says, **"It is sown a natural body; it is raised a spiritual body. If there is a natural body, there is also a spiritual body." Our bodies will be raised imperishable.** 1 Corinthians 15:42 says, "So it is with the resurrection of the dead.

What is sown is perishable; what is raised is imperishable." 1 Corinthians 15:52–54 repeats this promise.

So these verses reveal the permanent future of species—God's purpose for creating the world and the universe. The earth renewed will be the old earth redeemed and renewed without sin and/or sin's effects.

We have stated that the chief end of man is to glorify God and enjoy Him forever (Westminster Confession of Faith). The ultimate end of man is likewise to glorify God and enjoy Him forever. But this ultimate end is a reality: "every knee shall bow to Me, and every tongue shall confess to God" (Romans 14:11). (Also see Isaiah 45:23.) This worship and confession will not be a burden but an everlasting joy.

CHAPTER 33

The Alternative to Heaven

*Whoever undertakes to set himself up as a judge
of Truth and Knowledge is shipwrecked by the
laughter of the gods. Albert Einstein, 1954, 120*

THE ALTERNATIVE TO THE NEW heaven and new earth, according to the Bible, is hell. There are many verses in the Bible that speak of hell as a real place, reserved for all who do not accept Jesus Christ as their Lord and Savior. Here are a few from the book of Matthew: "whoever says, 'You fool!' will be liable to the hell of fire" (Matthew 5:22); "Rather fear Him Who can destroy both soul and body in hell" (Matthew 10:28); "It is better for you to enter life with one eye than with two eyes to be thrown into the hell of fire" (Matthew 18: 9)."

Jesus said this in Luke 16:22–31:

> The poor man died and was carried by the angels to Abraham's side. The rich man also died and was buried, and in Hades, being in torment, he lifted up his eyes and saw Abraham far off and Lazarus at his side. And he called out "Father Abraham, have mercy on me, and send Lazarus to dip the end of his finger in water and cool my tongue, for I am in anguish in this flame." But Abraham said, "Child, remember that you in your lifetime received your good things, and Lazarus in like matter bad things; but now he is comforted here, and you are in anguish. And besides all this,

between us and you a great chasm has been fixed, in order that those who pass from here to you may not be able, and none may cross from there to us." And he said, "Then I beg you, father, to send him to my father's house—for I have five brothers—so that he may warn them, lest they also come into this place of torment." But Abraham said, "They have Moses and the Prophets; let them hear them." And he said, "No, father Abraham, but if someone goes to them from the dead, they will repent." He said to him, "If they do not hear Moses and the Prophets, neither will they be convinced if someone should rise from the dead."

These verses from Jesus are very descriptive of heaven and its relationship to sinners. Heaven is an exclusive place, reserved for those who truly believe in the Lord Jesus, who have been born again—not by the will of man but by the will of God—and can therefore coexist with a holy God.

In 2 Peter 2:4 we read, "For if God did not spare angels when they sinned, but cast them into hell and committed them to chains of gloomy darkness to be kept until the judgment." In Revelation 1:18, Jesus said, "I have the keys of Death and Hades;" and Revelation 20:13–15 says, "Death and Hades gave up the dead who were in them, and they were judged, each one of them, according to what they had done. Then Death and Hades were thrown into the lake of fire. This is the second death, the lake of fire. And if anyone's name was not found written in the book of life, he was thrown into the lake of fire."

So the alternative to heaven is hell, and each of us has an opportunity to choose. Don't pity those who reject Jesus. As Abraham said, they had the chance to believe God's Word, and they rejected it. There are two options besides justice: injustice and mercy; God grants mercy and never injustice. It is not justice for someone who continues to deny Jesus, and is therefore unholy, to be saved by Jesus's blood and to become a child of God. Then God's holiness would be destroyed. You can argue that God's holiness cannot be destroyed, and that is true because God will allow no one unholy in His presence.

Most Christians seem to believe in assurance of salvation: once saved, always saved—perseverance of the saints. But some, when asked if they are going to heaven, will answer, "Well, I hope so." In other words they don't know; they might go to heaven, or they might go to hell. **How we spend eternity is the biggest issue in our lives. This time on the earth is insignificant compared to our time in Heaven or Hell.**

There are many verses in the Bible that speak of whether we are saved:

- "And this is the will of Him Who sent Me, that I should lose nothing of all that He has given Me, but raise it up on the last day" (John 6:39).
- John 10:28–30 says, concerning Jesus's sheep, "I give them eternal life, and they will never perish, and no one will snatch them out of My hand. My Father, Who has given them to Me, is greater than all, and no one is able to snatch them out of the Father's hand. I and the Father are one."
- "And I am sure of this, that He who began a good work in you will bring it to completion at the day of Jesus Christ" (Philippians 1:6).
- I write these things to you who believe in the name of the Son of God that you may know that you have eternal life" (1 John 5:13).

And we read this in Hebrews 3:16–19:

For who were those who heard and yet rebelled? Was it not all those who left Egypt led by Moses? And with whom was He provoked for forty years? Was it not with those who sinned, whose bodies fell in the wilderness? And to whom did He swear that they would not enter His rest, but to those who were disobedient? So we see that they were unable to enter because of unbelief.

So we know that we are saved if we believe in Jesus! What does *believe* mean? According to Webster's it means "to have a firm religious faith, to accept trustfully and on faith, to have a firm conviction as to the reality or goodness of something." **We should therefore know, without a doubt, whether we will go to heaven or hell if we believe God's Word.** Salvation is absolutely sure because it is of God from the beginning to the end. John 10:25–28 says, "Jesus answered them 'I told you, and you do not believe. The works that I do in My Father's name bear witness about Me, but you do not believe because you are not among My sheep. My sheep hear My voice, and I know them, and they follow Me. I give them eternal life, and they will never perish."

We must believe in Jesus and all He said with the faith of a little child. We must be willing to give up everything if it should come to that—our family, our riches, our friends, our very life—because we believe so strongly in Jesus. So there are questions we can ask ourselves: How far am I willing to go for Jesus? How big is my God? Can He really do what He says? Do I have faith in Him and trust in Him? Do I have a firm conviction of the reality and goodness of Jesus? Do I even believe in a supernatural God and His miracles? **If we can answer these questions positively, we do believe, and we are going to heaven.** *No one is able to snatch us away!* **(John 10:29).**

CHAPTER 34
The Interim Future of Species

I have never imputed to Nature a purpose or a goal, or anything that could be understood as anthropomorphic. What I see in Nature is a magnificent structure that we can comprehend only very imperfectly, and that must fill a thinking person with a feeling of humility. This is a genuinely religious feeling that has nothing to do with mysticism. Albert Einstein, 1954, 208

THE ULTIMATE FUTURE OF SPECIES is settled: heaven or hell. If there is a supernatural reality, we as humans are part of that supernatural reality and can't be separated by death. Death of organics is the end of natural reality. We are ultimately converted into carbon dioxide and water, just as the pile of dog feces in our lawn.

In the case of a supernatural reality—not observed by our five senses but existing in our hearts and souls—even more real than a natural reality, there is no beginning and, therefore, no end; there is no death. So our souls must supernaturally exist in some form. Science is unqualified to explain this, but theology can.

The weakness of theology is that there are no theological laws that humans can discover and document. The strength of theology is that the invincible Head of both the natural and the supernatural worlds claims that He has transcribed certain spiritual laws that apply in both worlds and that supersede the natural laws, which were only discovered by man, but were established by his Ceator.

We can theoretically prove natural laws by ourselves, and therefore they seem more believable to us. Spiritual laws do not depend on the adequacy of man's proof and belief; they are written by God—the head of the supernatural—and they are true, regardless of man's imperfect judgment.

We have an unknown amount of time between the present and the ultimate future, according to the Bible. So our position as humans is to do our part, large or small, to make that interim future pleasant for our loved ones and ourselves.

We should work to return God's fallen creation to its natural, original state—with the exception that we have been given the direction *to be fruitful and multiply*, and our very existence changes that original state. We have concurrently been given the direction to have dominion and responsibility over that creation. We must conclude that since God created the world and its supporting universe and said it was *good*, if we don't preserve the world as created, it will be less than *good*. Therefore our sacred duty is to examine God's description of the original Creation and insist that it be retained in its original *goodness* as it populates further.

One fatal mistake that nature worshipers make is to assume that humans are not part of nature. We are not only part of nature, but also the reason for nature. There would be no purpose for nature, if not for humans. When God gave us directions *to be fruitful and multiply*, He put no limit on the multiplication. Apparently, the earth is large enough to sustain the population until the time of its conversion into the New Earth and the New Heaven, so we should have no concern about overpopulation. If you have ever been to the midwestern states, you understand.

We have no obligation to preserve human-created organics, machines, or structures, except for practical, natural reasons. But *nature* is to be protected. **Nature does not diminish as population grows; it is only replaced by a higher form of creation. This speaks to our concern**

about extinction of species. That extinction is happening every day; it always has, and it must continue, as the higher form of species—humans—replaces the lower forms. As long as vegetation and subhuman animal species are preserved to the extent that human life can be sustained, as was the original purpose of Creation, our dominion responsibility will be successful. **Nature was not created exclusively for our enjoyment, or the enjoyment of an initiated few, but primarily for our sustenance. The purpose of our enjoyment of nature is for it to witness to its Creator in beauty, perfection, wonder, respect, worship, and sometimes even fear!** Nature was not created for our worship, as Einstein said above, but for our worship of its Creator.

So we do not have an option; we must work to maintain the inorganic and organic balance of our earth. Man has the knowledge and power today, and will even more so in the future, to maintain civilization as it was created with its mandated growth.

As is obvious to most people today, the natural law of entropy applies to humans as well as to other forms of nature. (Books such as George Orwell's *1984*, written in 1949, and William Golding's *Lord of the Flies*, written in 1954 predicted this.) Left alone, we will degrade ourselves into chaos. Selfishness and sin will prevail in humans just as disorder prevails in all nature. **Thankfully, we were not—and are not—left alone!**

Our Interim Needs

God has created a world that provides for our needs and always will until He calls us home. He has done that not only with His creation of nature but with His instructions in the Bible that give direction to civilization. God gave us marriage, the basis for families, and the growth and order established therein. He gave us the Ten Commandments, the basis for civilized law. He gave us the organization for a theocratic government, which was the basis for English law and now US law. He gave us graphic examples of good and bad leaders and the results of that leadership. He gave us the command to work hard and provide for our families and for those who can't provide for themselves. And above all, He gave us—through Jesus—the radical concepts of humility, righteousness, compassion, love, mercy, purity, and peace. (See Matthew 5:2–12.)

So what are our real needs? We can survive with adequate food, clothing, and shelter, but in the United States we have a Constitutional Bill of Rights. These "rights" are mostly freedoms from, and representation before, the federal government—not needs for survival or even comfort. Over the last 150 years, the federal government has decided that citizens are *entitled* to certain additional benefits from the government, including retirement income, education, minimum wages, public health, public safety, protection from big business, the use of public lands for recreation, food quality, pharmaceutical approval, control of agriculture, labor practices, housing, energy, transportation, civil rights, and many others.

In the future we will need to decide which needs are to be provided by the federal government, which by state or local governments, and which by charities. Rights for some people are intrusions for others. Some people are independent and prefer to be free of all benefits and controls, while others are—or are encouraged to be—more dependent. Since the federal government is not an income producer, it must depend on involuntary contributions from its constituents to fund its programs and pay its expenses. According to Forbes Opinion, in an article posted on the website on July 2, 2014, 35.5 percent of people in the United States received government benefits that did not include social security. The percent before social Security benefits which are paid in by employees and employers, is 49.2. Approximately 14 percent of all jobs are for federal, state, or local governments.[1] These figures should be additive, assuming that government workers are compensated well enough to be ineligible for benefits. **Therefore, approximately 49.5 percent of the US population is dependent on the other half for their needs. This appears to be unsustainable, since for every hour one person works, one half of that person's income goes to others, with only one half remaining for personal use.** The only solution to this dilemma is for there to be significantly fewer government employees or fewer entitlements.

Of the needs, benefits, and entitlements listed above, certain pertain more to one demographic category than others. For instance, young people are interested in education and jobs, middle-aged people are interested in children's education and job improvement, and older people are more focused on retirement and heath benefits. **It is critical in the future to develop a fair and equitable system for all demographics without penalizing those who are higher income earners, and thereby stagnating ambition, growth, and new job opportunities.**

Should We Agree to Disagree?

This is a valid question that is considered today to be the end of all arguments, and unfortunately, it is the end of all learning. If two sides disagree on natural questions, the easiest solution is to agree to disagree—just go our separate ways, with each side feeling right. But each view may be right, or it may be wrong. God's creation is so complex that we will never understand it all. If we did, we would be God. But we can keep learning and keep trying to discern the truth of nature.

If we agree to disagree on spiritual questions, this cop-out is not so reasonable and valid. Our responsibility, especially when confronted with a spiritual disagreement, is to try to discover the truth through researching the Bible. Commentaries and books will certainly help, but as said previously, the Bible is not confusing because God is not confusing. If we can't understand a spiritual truth, it is likely because we have either given up, or we are not prayerfully asking the Holy Spirit to help. He is called the Helper for a real reason. Granted, we can never understand all truths, or we would have Adam and Eve's problem, but we can understand what God wants us to understand. Then faith takes over, and we believe.

If our goal in life is to avoid conflicts and to limit our intellectual growth to its present state, then agreeing to disagree is a satisfactory resolution. But the simple fact is that when two people,

or two sides, disagree one is usually wrong, and many times both are wrong. It is impossible to logically prove that there are multiple truths. There are always multiple solutions but never multiple truths. It is invalid to say, "If it's true for you, that's OK, but it's not true for me." There is one God, and He is Truth. All truth is God's truth. (See Isaiah 45:19; John 15:26, 16:13, 8:32; 2 Corinthians 2:8; and 2 Thessalonians 2:10.) So our responsibility is to learn the truth, whether we have to lose an argument or not. When we cease to do that, we cease to grow, and our future is bleak.

When we have a deep conviction in an issue, based on experience, study and prayer, and a family member or loved one disagees, we must still love them but make it very clear that we do not approve of their choice. I believe that God has established family relationships as He established marriage, to never be broken. Tough love should not include kicking a child out of the house, or ceasing to communicate.

In the last one hundred years, we have largely displaced truth, and substituted information. Information and knowledge have become our biggest industry—and truth its most spectacular victim.[2]

I certainly do not say that my opinions as expressed in this book are scientifically or Biblically perfect, but I have done my best to understand scientific advances and to discern God's truth as expressed in the Bible. I simply want to challenge the reader to think critically and research and pray on his own so that God will reveal the truth.

WILL WE BE LIBERAL OR CONSERVATIVE?

These are terms that our politicians and media have stolen and applied to enemies as an ugly characterization. *Webster's Dictionary* defines *liberal* as "broad minded" and *conservative* as "traditional." There are different categories of though, and most people will admit that they are liberal in some and conservative in others. For instance, there are social values—but these range from abortion, to minority rights, to minority treatment, to marriage, to health care, to war, to criminal justice, to the death penalty, to care for the poor, and on and on. Fiscal values range from national debt, to minimum wage, to the tax system, to redistribution of wealth. Political values consider the size, services, and abuses of the federal government, overreach of government branches, state's rights, socialism versus free enterprise, property rights, and more. Religious values include abortion, euthanasia, marriage, tax exemption, freedom of speech, and others.

To resolve these issues in the future, we must be both conservative and liberal; we must study and learn from history and be open to improvement.

Most people would prefer that all responses to our values be fair and equitable to everyone concerned. But the interpretation of fairness differs, depending on how it affects you. Jesus taught a perfect, but hard, solution to our beliefs and actions in the Sermon on the Mount. If we are truly poor in spirit (recognize that we need God's help), if we mourn (because of our sin), if we are meek (gentle), if we hunger and thirst for righteousness, if we are merciful, pure in heart, peacemakers, if we are persecuted for righteousness sake, and if we are persecuted for belief in Jesus, we will be blessed (Matthew 5:2–11). Can we meet this difficult challenge in the future? The answer is that we cannot without God, just as we can't meet the intent of the Ten Commandments. But with the power of the Holy Spirit, which dwells in us if we believe and trust in God, we can be all of this. Then there will be no need to categorize ourselves as conservative or liberal. Jesus was a radical liberal socially and religiously, a staunch biblical conservative, and when He, as the Word, inspired the words of the Old Testament, spoke clearly and conservatively about fiscal and government issues. He never wavered in the truth of the inerrancy of the scripture.

So we have a model and the power to personally be above politics and labels in the future, but it will take God's intervention for others to see the truth.

The End Times

At some time in the future, before heaven on earth, the Bible predicts that Jesus Christ will return to this earth. Since Jesus Himself spoke of the end times, it is proper to start with His words from Matthew 24:15–27:

> So when you see the abomination of desolation spoken of by the prophet Daniel, standing in the holy place (let the reader understand), then let those who are in Judea flee to the mountains. Let the one who is on the housetop not go down to take what is in the house, and let the one who is in the field not turn back to take his cloak. And alas for women who are pregnant and for those who are nursing infants in those days! Pray that your flight may not be in winter or on a Sabbath. For then there shall be great tribulation, such as has not been from the beginning of the world until now, no, and never will be. And if those days had not been cut short, no human being would be saved. But for the sake of the elect those days will be cut short. Then if anyone says to you, "Look, here is the Christ!" or "There He is!" do not believe it. For false christs and false prophets will arise and perform great signs and wonders, so as to lead astray, if possible, even the elect. See, I have told you beforehand. So, if they say to you, "Look, He is in the wilderness," do not go out. If they say, "Look, He is in the inner rooms," do not believe it. For as the lightening comes from the east and shines as far as the west, so will be the coming of the Son of Man.

Jesus is referring to Daniel 9:22–27, 11:31 and 12:11–13. **Jesus did not waste His words on confusing prophesies but spoke only the truth, and no one in His lifetime, or since, has ever successfully disputed His words. We deny them at our risk!**

In 1 Thessalonians 4:13–18, Paul gave us an idea of how Christians who are alive in the end times will be saved from the tribulations described in the Book of Revelation:

> But we do not want you to be uninformed, brothers, about those who are asleep, that you may not grieve as others do who have no hope. For since we believe that Jesus died and rose again, even so, through Jesus, God will bring with Him those who have fallen asleep. For this we declare to you by a word from the Lord, that we who are alive, who are left until the coming of the Lord, will not precede those who have fallen asleep. For the Lord Himself will descend from heaven with a cry of command, with the voice of an archangel, and with the sound of the trumpet of God. And the dead in Christ will rise first. Then we who are alive, who are left, will be caught up together with them in the clouds to meet the Lord in the air, and so we will always be with the Lord. Therefore encourage one another with these words.

Those who recognize that God is not constrained by time, as discussed in chapter 11, will not be surprised at the prophecy that the dead will all apparently rise together, closely followed by the last survivors. There is no indication that those arriving first in heaven will be on a higher plane, or shown more respect or reverence. It appears that all Christians will be shown into heaven at the same time (since there is no time at all there). Remember, it is God Who calls us to heaven, not our works or our time of death. **Praise God, though, that we will at last not only be reunited with our loved ones and our offspring forever, but with all the saints of history to worship God together. We don't have to worry about whether we will get bored with continuous worship, we will be reconstituted, perfect beings, ready, and available to do whatever God wants.**

Paul spoke these inspired words in 2 Thessalonians 2:1–12:

> Now concerning the coming of our Lord Jesus Christ and our being gathered together to Him, we ask you, brothers, not to be quickly shaken in mind or alarmed, either by a spirit or a spoken

word, or letter seeming to come from us, to the effect that the day of the Lord has come. Let no one deceive you in any way. For that day will not come, unless the rebellion comes first, and the man of lawlessness is revealed, the son of destruction, who opposes and exalts himself against every so-called god or object of worship, so that he takes his seat in the temple of God, proclaiming himself to be God. Do you not remember that when I was still with you I told you these things? And you know what is restraining Him now so He may be revealed in His time. For the mystery of lawlessness is already at work. Only He who now restrains it will do so until he is out of the way. And then the lawless one will be revealed, whom the Lord Jesus will kill with the breath of His mouth and bring to nothing by the appearance of His coming. The coming of the lawless one is by the activity of Satan with all power and false signs and wonders, and for all wicked deception for those who are perishing, for they refused to love the truth and so be [saved]. Therefore God sends them a strong delusion, so that they may believe what is false, in order that all may be condemned who did not believe the truth but had pleasure in unrighteousness.

John in Revelation 6–20 gives detailed descriptions of the events prophesized in Daniel and other places that will occur during the end times before Christ returns.

---

1 Merrill Matthews, *Forbes/ Opinion, We've Crossed The Tipping Point; Most Americans Now Receive Government Benefits*, July 2,2014
2 Arch Warren, *Jesus, light and Truth* (Nashville, TN: Covenant Presbyterian Church). 2015

Part 2
The Future through Evolution

CHAPTER 35
Introduction

I'm a magnet for all the crackpots in the world, but they are of interest to me too. A favorite pastime of mine is to reconstruct their thinking process. I feel genuinely sorry for them, that's why I try to help them. Albert Einstein, 1953, 14

DARWIN EXTRAPOLATED HIS THEORIES INTO the future by stating the following:

> We can so far take a prophetic glance into futurity as to foretell that it will be the common and widely spread species, belonging to the larger and dominant groups, which will ultimately prevail and procreate new and dominant species. As all the living forms of life are the lineal descendants of those which lived long before the Silurian epoch, we may feel certain that the ordinary succession by generation has never once been broken, and that no cataclysm has desolated the whole world. Hence we may look with some confidence to a secure future of equally inappreciable length. And as natural selection works solely by and for the good of each being, all corporal and mental endowments will tend to progress towards perfection.[1]

So much for the law of entropy!

Will we transfer our personalities or mindfiles into robots, leaving our violent, unsustainable bodies behind,[2] or rather than literal robots, will we become human robots controlled by the government rather than God?

Evolution does not know, and cannot tell us, what the future holds. However, I will present Pierre Teilhard's prospective in the following chapter. Teilhard is one of the more serious and accepted evolutionary thinkers, and we will explore his future-of-mankind predictions from a theistic evolutionary perspective.

---

[1] Charles Darwin, "Recapitulation and Conclusion," in *The Origin of Species*, 399.
[2] Ray Waddle, *The Tennessean, Message of the Week, Contemplating Future of the Soul*, June 20, 2015,

CHAPTER 36

The Omega Point

Strenuous intellectual work and the study of God's nature are the angels that will lead me through all the troubles of this life with consolation, strength, and uncompromising rigor. Albert Einstein, 1897, 3

As we consider the future through the eyes of evolution, it is important to understand what the influential evolutionary thinkers have predicted. I don't think it is of real value to spend time with the works of authors such as Carl Sagan, an astronomer and cosmologist; Stephen Hawking, a theoretical physicist and cosmologist; or Richard Dawkins, an evolutionary biologist. Their experience is too specialized, and their biases too entrenched for them to be of real interest. But there are several evolutionary deeper thinkers who are worth reading. For instance, Pierre Teilhard was quoted extensively in chapter 7 and is worth revisiting because of his predictions for the future. He coined the term *point Omega* in his *The Future of Mankind*, chapter 6, section IV:

> We are enabled…by the idea…that…in the heart of, a universe prolonged along the axis of complexity, there exists a divine center of convergence…let us call it the point Omega…A phenomenon perhaps outwardly akin to death; but in reality a simple metamorphosis and arrival at the supreme synthesis. An escape from the

planet, not in space or outwardly, but spiritually and inwardly, such as the hypercentration of cosmic matter upon itself allows.[1]

In the "Note by French Editor" at the end of the book, Teilhard is quoted from as early as 1916 from *La Vie Cosmique, which shows the unity of fundamental Christian vision and scientific knowledge that he preserved to the end.* Among these quotes is this one: "And since the time Jesus was born, when he finished growing and died and rose again, everything has continued to move because Christ has not yet attained His full growth. In the pursuance of this engendering is situated the ultimate spring of all created activity…Christ is the fulfillment eve of the natural evolution of beings."

Teilhard was a Jesuit priest and professor of geology at the Catholic Institute in Paris, Director of the National Geologic Survey of China, and Director of the National Research Center of France. Many of his theories do not conform to those of Christianity, and many of his writings were censored by the church in his lifetime, but as the Vatican spokesman Fr. Federico Lombardi said in 2009, "By now no one would dream of saying that [Teilhard] is a heterodox author who shouldn't be studied."

This valuable work is an example of why all views in science and religion should be open to study. **I believe that there is no danger in exposing people, even children of an appropriate age, to divergent thoughts *as long as* opposing thoughts are presented equally. This is the sad and unjust antithesis of today's educational establishment's refusal to allow the teaching of scientific creationism (not an oxymoron).**

---

[1] Pierre Teilhard de Chardin, *The Future of Mankind* (return to religion-online, 1959).

CHAPTER 37

Reliance on Science as We Move into the Future

§

I have no special talents. I am only passionately curious. Albert Einstein, 1952, 14

IN THE NATURAL WORLD, IT is important to consider the latest research into a scientific issue because of the legitimate assumption that with time and effort, we will understand more about the truth of natural reality. In fact, as a scientist, my entire career has been based on this assumption. But in the realm of the supernatural, time and effort are irrelevant. There is no reason that we will understand more about the supernatural with time or effort, unless we grow spiritually and spend time and effort prayerfully studying God's Word.

Reliance on scientific research and publications is critical to the practice of natural science, but to understand ultimate truth, the only publication of real value is the Holy Bible, and the only legitimate research into ultimate truth is study of that Word.

As we prepare for the interim future before the return of Jesus, it is critical that we do not fall into the trap of accepting an unproven theory such as evolution as fact. It is especially alarming that such a theory is taught in school systems as fact, with no attempt at confirming the theory or questioning its lack of scientific proof. Our society has lied to and misled several generations into believing a fantasy. Consequently, the imbedded belief that so many unthinking people today have in macroevolution is responsible for much of the devaluation of life, in the form of abortion acceptance, the rise of murder, terrorism, and crime committed by young people, and the acceptance of euthanasia and assisted suicide. When society does not hold a person responsible for his actions, as evolution teaches, the society will fail. This happened in ancient Greece, Rome, and more recently in Nazi Germany and Communist Russia, and it is in the process of happening in the United States.

CHAPTER 38
Can Our Art and Science Advance?

Although I am a typical loner in my daily life, my awareness of belonging to the invisible community of those who strive for truth, beauty, and justice has prevented me from feelings of isolation. Albert Einstein, 1932, 11

As HARD AS IT IS to admit, even though we have more natural information available than at any time in history, because of the natural law of entropy—that the net energy in the universe diminishes with time—we have less intelligence and ability to understand that information. This law of entropy as it concerns our ability as an individual is heresy to a typical scientist, who assumes—in order to make his or her life's work relevant—that science will discover the source and explanation for everything, natural and supernatural (if one accept the supernatural at all).

In addition to the law of entropy, most will admit that today we don't have an Archimedes, Boyle, Einstein, Joules, Newton, or Pascal practicing science. In the arts there is no Bach, Beethoven, Brahms, or Mozart—no Monet, Homer, Da Vinci, or Michelangelo. Despite vastly increased communication, no one today is able to create beauty in the arts as people once did. In theology, where are the Martin Luthers, the John Calvins, the C. S. Lewises, the Matthew Henrys, and the Francis Schaffers? **Mankind seems to have lost the ability to be great—or is it just entropy at work, an irreversible devolution of intelligence and wisdom? We are**

inundated with knowledge and facts with inadequate response. Not only have we almost lost greatness, the population of the world has lost the ability to recognize and appreciate greatness. I am deliberately mentioning great scientists and artists from radically different generations to demonstrate that we still have greatness, but more rarely. It seems that the more lasting and deeper work is the older work. It could be argued that the easier scientific work was done in the past, and only the more difficult remains. The same could be said for music, visual art, literature, and theology. But if you understand the complexity of the natural world, and especially the spiritual world, you can see that both are virtually infinite, and that we will never reach a void of exciting discovery. This is especially true in science and theology, the subjects of this book, but also true in the arts. After all, what is art but what *Webster's* says: "the skill acquired by experience, study or observation"?

I believe that we have been able to realize scientific advancement, in spite of the acceptance of very few new laws in the last few generations, because we have the research, testing, and calculating tools to manipulate facts more than ever before. Witness the discovery of DNA, genes, and genomes, which has started a relatively new science that has helped to prove Creation and has virtually destroyed the belief in macroevolution.

The members of our scientific community are becoming engineers instead of scientists, manipulating laws and facts and simply applying them in different and imaginary ways. This is all necessary to advance prosperity, but it does not lead us to radical improvements to face the future in a world split by political, religious, and racial walls. Our artists and authors are building experimental monuments to themselves to shock and titillate, instead of bringing viewers and readers to peace and joy, while countless natural facts, sound and rhythm possibilities, visual depictions, literature ideas in fact and fiction, and spiritual truths remain to be discovered and developed.

Part 3
How We Can Affect the Future

CHAPTER 39

The Future of Wealth, Jobs, and Education

I am absolutely convinced that no amount of wealth can help humanity forward, even in the hands of the most dedicated worker in this cause. The example of great and pure personalities can lead us to noble deeds and views. Money only appeals to selfishness, and, without fail, it tempts its owner to abuse it. Can anyone imagine Moses, Jesus, or Gandhi with the moneybags of Carnegie? Albert Einstein, 1932, 283

WEALTH ACCUMULATION OR DISTRIBUTION

MANY SECULAR—AND SOME RELIGIOUS—teachers, communicators, and politicians today consider economic equality a critical need for the survival of species. The accepted solution of economic equality seems to be a redistribution of wealth. There are three ways to obtain wealth: to steal or take by force or deceit, to work for it, or to receive it freely. In a socialistic government, everyone—regardless of education, talents, or hard work—is theoretically granted equal wealth (except, of course, the administrators who receive certain additional benefits such as expense accounts, housing, protection, education, and travel in order to manage others efficiently). Then all income is shared evenly between the remaining citizens, and they are assured of certain necessities, such as food, clothing, shelter, medical care, education, retirement, entertainment, and recreational drugs.

Some Christians have referred to the practice of the early church, in order to rationalize this approach to equalize the masses.

> Now the full number of those who believed were of one heart and soul, and no one said that any of the things that belonged to him was his own, but they had everything in common. And with great power the apostles were giving their testimony to the resurrection of the Lord Jesus, and grace was upon them all. There was not a needy person among them, for as many as were owners of lands or houses sold them and brought the proceeds of what was sold and laid it at the apostles' feet, and it was distributed to each as any had need (Acts 4:32–35).

(See also Acts 2:43–44, 5:1–11, and 2 Corinthians 8: 13–15.)

But these words, instead, speak to the church's responsibility to see that none in the church has any need. If all churches would really practice this, think of the blessings to the congregants and the savings to the government. Jesus teaches that charity should be voluntary and apply to all believers. A common criticism that church and government charities share is that many times they give with an expectation. Jesus taught giving out of grace with no expectations.

Chapter 32 describes the New Heaven in which there will be no need for a redistribution of wealth because there will be no wealth, other than the real wealth of a permanent relationship with God.

In this world, the early church—which was touched by the Holy Spirit on the day of Pentecost and was led by the apostles and disciples who were taught directly by Jesus Christ—was able to exist in harmony and economic equality for a period of time. (Note the problems that occurred later in the churches as described in 1 Corinthians 3 and Revelation 2–3.) But in the world today, cursed in Genesis 3:17–19 to work in pain and sweat and then to die, there will always be those who are unable mentally or physically to provide for their own needs. Unfortunately, regardless of good intentions, governments will always be unqualified to lead a society benevolently because of man's sin nature apart from God.

JOBS

So can the future bring an economic equality? Should it be our goal, or our government's goal, to take from the rich and distribute to the poor? Is it fair to take from a person who has worked and sacrificed all of his or her life and give to a person who refuses to work or take risks? Should any amount of hard work, education, or ability deserve more pay? When these questions are asked and answered, the impossibility of managing a system that is fair to all is clear. It is possible that a church can accomplish this goal through spiritual wisdom, but in a secular government, it is impossible. All past socialist governments have failed or are rapidly deteriorating.

That is why Paul, especially, made such a point of working for his sustenance, why Jesus worked as a carpenter, and why all of the apostles had jobs and ministered on the side. (See 1 Corinthians 9, 1 Thessalonians 4:11, 5:14, and 2 Thessalonians 3:6–9.)

The issue in the Bible verses above is not about money. The verses concern providing for the needs of those who are able to work and the needs of those who are unable to earn for themselves. Money is neither good nor evil, but it is an issue worth considering, since the Bible says, "For the love of money is a root of all kinds of evils" (1 Timothy 6:10). (See also Ecclesiastes 5:10, Matthew 6:24, Acts 8:20, 1 Timothy 3:3 and Hebrews 13:5). **Money is better than no money since it is our system of barter, and it should be used for good, for our needs, for our education, and even for sinless pleasures. But it is not the score in the game of life.** Jesus accumulated money, and He and his group of disciples had money when needed to fund their ministry and provide for their needs. His use of money should be our example. When Jesus lacked money, as in the stories of feeding the five thousand and the four thousand, the need was met through a miracle, just as it can be today.

The largest single measure of economic equality for the future will be job availability and acceptance. The "Frequently Asked Questions" page at SBA.gov currently says that 99.7 percent of employers in the United States have less than five hundred employees and are, therefore, classified as small businesses. Small businesses provided 64 percent of new private-sector jobs and 49.2 percent of private-sector employment. The latest information from SBA in 2015 lists small-business jobs at 70 percent now and new jobs at 60–80 percent. In the future, effort should be made to assure that this small-business economy driver receives equal treatment to large businesses and that the ease of starting a new business is considered with all regulations. Today, congressional legislation—and especially federal administrative edicts—have been extremely unfair to small businesses.

What about stratification within the private and the public sectors of employment? Should the future have no masters, no slaves, no servants, no bosses, and no workers? The Bible says that positions are irrelevant; we should be satisfied in our circumstances. (See Ephesians 6:16 and 1 Thessalonians 5:18.) **If every person treated every other person fairly, positions in this world would not matter. It is positional abuse, either way, which causes injustice.** (See Colossians 3:23–25 and 4:1.) 1 Timothy 6:1–10 explains it this way:

> Let all who are under a yoke as bondservants regard their own masters as worthy of all honor, so that the name of God and the teaching may not be reviled. Those who have believing masters must not be disrespectful on the grounds that they are brothers; rather they must serve all the better since those who benefit by their good service are believers and beloved. Teach and urge these things. If anyone teaches a different doctrine and does not agree with the sound words of our Lord Jesus Christ and the teaching that accords with godliness, he is puffed up with conceit and understands nothing. He has an unhealthy craving for controversy

and for quarrels about words, which produce envy, dissention, slander, evil suspicions, and constant friction among people who are depraved in mind and deprived of the truth, imagining that godliness is a means of gain. But godliness with contentment is great gain, for we brought nothing into the world, and we cannot take anything out of the world. But if we have food and clothing, with these we will be content. But those who desire to be rich fall into temptation, into a snare, into many senseless and harmful desires that plunge people into ruin and destruction. For the love of money is a root of all kinds of evils. It is through this craving that some have wandered away from the faith and pierced themselves with many pangs.

This passage contains harsh words for those who follow hate acts around the country with an unhealthy *craving for controversy*.

Paul says, "If we have food and clothing, with these we will be content." We don't have to enjoy excessive food and clothing to be content, but we as Christians must see that none of our flock has inadequate food and clothing. This is one of those exciting teachings in the Bible that can comfort and bless but that some will make a religion around and abuse.

The types of available jobs will likely radically change in the interim future. As information technology takes over the jobs for which people are now being trained, rather than educated, education will become even more important. And that education will change to become more thinking and reasoning oriented, rather than implementation oriented. People will be taught to be innovators and leaders, instead of just doers. It is probable that computers will replace many of the professional jobs. This could well include engineering, accounting, law, and even portions of dentistry and medicine. For instance, with nanotechnology, it is possible to operate and/or cure medically by injecting nanobots in the bloodstream that are not much larger than viruses such as cancer.

But there will be many other new positions that will open up or expand. These should include the jobs requiring critical thinking, such as teaching, research, upper management, and those service jobs supporting the business and leisure activities. These should include consulting, computer science, hospitality, recreation, sports, food, clothing, and shelter. In order to prepare future generations for these jobs, education must revise its emphasis from training for specific professions to a more general approach of mastering reading, writing, and arithmetic—as well as art, history, critical thinking, reason, and logic. As Einstein was quoted above, "Imagination is more important than knowledge." **Computers can provide almost unlimited knowledge, but only the wise can use that knowledge to advance civilization.** In the future it will be even more important for younger people to look ahead before deciding on a career.

Taxes

For those who work, taxes have always been a source of dissatisfaction and have been used as a tool for redistribution of the wealth. There are three main sources of taxation: income, property, and sales. Historically, the federal government has used income tax; the states, sales tax; and the municipalities, property taxes. Governments have been innovative in developing new areas of taxation in forms such as fuel, business privilege, business licenses, and inheritance. The federal tax code has become extremely complicated since income is difficult to determine, and businesses and other special interests spend so much on influencing the tax code. There is a false idea that high-income earners spend a lesser percent of their income, but—assuming no deductions, and even with no taxes on critical food, clothing, and shelter—the high-income earners actually spend a greater percent. There is no rational justification, other than punishment, to charge a higher tax rate to higher earners. Why should citizens be punished for success?

One fair and equitable resolution is to have only one tax in the form of a sales tax, paid by individuals, companies, churches, and everyone else to the seller—all as a percent of purchases. Lower, or no, tax could be charged for nonluxury foods, clothing, and shelter. The sales tax rate could be set annually by simply dividing the budget by the total amount of sales. Existing state-revenue departments could collect this tax, and a portion could be passed on to the federal and local governments. This would eliminate tax cheats, tax credits, tax preparation, and the threat the government has over religious and conservative schools, churches, and organizations. A decision would have to be made as to whether tax-exempt organizations would be exempt from sales tax as they are now. It may be best for them to pay sales taxes also, since they benefit from governmental services. The IRS could then be abandoned, along with the cost of tax returns.

EDUCATION

In order to allow everyone who is physically and mentally able to have an opportunity to be employed and self-sustaining, those adults must be trained or educated to qualify for a job. One of the main questions concerning this issue is whether the government has the responsibility to provide the necessary education and, if so, how to determine who gets what education. In a socialist state, the rulers have the right to educate their children and to decide what others qualify for. This is also true with most monarchies. In the United States, the Constitution does not list education as a right, but most people realize that without education or training, society will naturally stratify by economics to a dangerous degree.

Since the Tenth Amendment of the US Constitution states that "the powers not delegated to the United States by the Constitution, nor prohibited by it to the States, are reserved to the States respectively, or to the people," the federal government has no educational authority. Even though, as in most services, the federal government has overstepped its bounds, schools are run almost exclusively by private, state, or municipality. Anyone can start a school, but the federal government, states, and/or municipalities have taken over the responsibility of regulating the quality of the school—with the exception of home and church-sponsored schools, which are theoretically independent of the government because of the First Amendment of the Constitution. It has been argued that the state or the federal government must approve the secular part of a home or church education. Remote control of education results in valuing the appearance of education, instead of education itself.

In the future—if there is freedom within these Constitutional bounds for schools to succeed or fail based on their ability to assure jobs or further education for their students and monopolies are prohibited—the quality of schools should improve. We must prevent using education as a social experiment to make students feel good and reserve the valuable school days for real learning or training. **Since citizens who elect to send their children to private schools should not be charged for an optional service not used, more families would be able to afford the education of their choice. It is a weak argument that the loss of private-school income to public schools damages the quality of public schools. There are too many examples of higher-quality small schools.** Also, there is no economy of scale in the larger school systems, since the cost of education is labor, facilities, and operations, which are all directly proportional to the number of students, discounting wasteful bureaucracy.

There should be no quality difference in private and public education, especially if the public schools are allowed to teach (describe, not indoctrinate) all major religions and the part in history they have played. This prohibition has meant that most public schools are only teaching part of the truth. It could be said that religion is a private belief and, therefore, should be taught privately or in the home. That would be true if religion were a fantasy, like evolution, which by some strange logic is allowed to be taught. But the premise of this book, and my deep conviction, is that religion is reality, even more so than nature. If this is true, education without including theology is pathetically partial. I am not speaking against public education but against the government edit that eliminates from public education the teaching of the greatest and most important part of reality.

It is very important not to eliminate public schools, or we will eliminate meaningful job opportunities for many. Private education is becoming unnecessarily expensive. There will always be expensive, elite private schools, but *private* is not synonymous with *expensive*. Church-sponsored schools prove that. Many, probably most, church-sponsored schools cost less than the tax-based, per-pupil cost of comparable public schools. I know that as a fact because I served for several years on the board of a church-sponsored private school that was started from nothing. Most parents should be able to afford a private education when the portion of their taxes funding public education is eliminated.

There must be an opportunity for those who prefer public schools and for those who would rather their tax money go to public schools. There must also be a *safety net* for the poor and for those who are physically or mentally incapable of attaining an education. The financing of this safety net is really the only justifiable public-tax-supported responsibility. Families should pay for the tuition of those students who do not fall in these categories, just as private tuition is paid. **If we are to catch back up with the rest of the world, it is critical that our public schools be released from federal or state control and returned to the local municipalities.** Competition between public- and private-school systems, along with a lack of governmental subsidy for either, will allow the best to survive.

Summary

As Einstein insinuated in the quote beginning this chapter, wealth is irrelevant within the bigger picture. So why do we spend our lives learning and working? The simple and biblical answer is so that we can support our families and ourselves and not have to burden others for our support.

In the Bible, as in Einstein's mind, wealth is not important to the future; comfort, joy, and freedom are. Education, jobs, and income are critically needed to provide for these future needs, as the Bible confirms. Wealth is the accumulation of money, resources, or possessions and may or may not provide comfort, joy, and freedom. The Bible speaks against hoarding in Luke 12:15–21, 33, and 34. The familiar parable of the rich, young ruler in Matthew 19:18–22 and Luke 18:18–30 makes it clear that Jesus wants trust and faith in Himself, rather than in anything of the world—including money and wealth. Of course it's not money, it's "the love of money" that is a false god. As Jesus said in Luke 18:24, "How difficult it is for those who have wealth to enter the kingdom of God!"

So the purpose of education and jobs is not to accumulate wealth for the future; that accumulation can even be a hindrance to our well-being and salvation.

CHAPTER 40
The Future of Racial Relations

While it is true that an inherently free and scrupulous person may be destroyed, such an individual can never be enslaved or used as a blind tool. Albert Einstein, 1950, 266.

THE BIBLE DOES NOT WASTE words on racial equality because racial equality should be so basic and obvious among Christians. In Genesis 41:50 Joseph married Asenath, the daughter of an Egyptian priest who was African. Numbers 12:1 records that Moses married a Cushite woman, who was also an African from the region of modern Ethiopia and Sudan. Jesus had non-Jews in His ancestry: Rahab and Ruth. We don't know the ancestry of many of the New Testament disciples, nor does it matter. We have no physical description of Jesus, or hardly any Bible characters outside of David and a few others. How many biographies or fictional writings have no physical descriptions of their leading characters? **In literature, only the Author of the Bible has the confidence to reveal characters without descriptions**.

As in the case of money and position, race is irrelevant in God's eyes—and should be in ours. God gives no directions for financial retribution for past racial injustice because finances mean nothing. Our responsibility is to treat all races equally and with respect and not to worry about the speck in our brother's eye (Matthew 7:4). It is not our responsibility to force the world to think as we do but to present the Gospel to the world.

It appears that, in the future, the states and municipalities must enforce racial equality in hiring. These challenges vary from state to state depending on immigration practices. There is no question that in God's eyes, there is no differentiation between races, but practically, there is a difference in people, in education, and intelligence, regardless of race or wealth. The state governments must take responsibility for all of its citizens, especially when they have not had the opportunities others have had. **The goal should be remedial training and teaching so that those who start behind have the opportunity to catch up.**

Some races, especially Native American and African American, have been treated unfairly in the recent past—perhaps not by us, but by people in our country. We have inherited a responsibility to be especially sensitive to their needs in the access to and opportunity for education.

CHAPTER 41
The Future of Marriage and Families

My father's ashes lie in Milan. I buried my mother here [Berlin] only a few days ago. My children are in Switzerland...I myself have journeyed everywhere continuously—a stranger everywhere...To a person like me it is ideal to feel at home anywhere with his loved ones. Albert Einstein, 1920, 6

Marriage

THE BIBLE SAYS THAT A marriage is between one man and one woman—not same sex, not multiple spouses, not with animals or vegetables. God created marriage at Creation as described in Genesis 1:27–28, as man and women *to be fruitful and multiply and fill the earth.* Jesus said in Matthew 19:4–5, "He answered, 'Have you not read that He Who created them from the beginning made them male and female, and said "Therefore a man shall leave his father and his mother and hold fast to his wife, and the two shall become one flesh"?'" So the original purpose of marriage was to be close to a spouse, to have children, and to teach the children the way they should go (Proverbs 22:6). God's model for a family has proven to function best from a practical standpoint. A child needs a mother to provide the tender love and nurture he or she cries for and must emulate, and a child needs a father to teach skills and perseverance to survive in society. These truths are difficult for someone who is not a Christian or

Jew to fathom—or for someone who does not accept the truth of Creation, since this person has no base for understanding the history of civilization.

Our governments have taken over the issuance of marriage licenses and added secular marriage services with no authority from the Initiator and Founder of marriage, the Lord God. God only ordained three institutions: marriage (family), church, and civil government. The church has allowed the travesty of the elimination of the purpose of the first of these institutions, and now secular marriages between those of the same sex are allowed in the United States—and all states are forced to recognize these biblically illegal marriages. There is no end to this blasphemy; in the future, gender, age, kin, number, animal, or vegetable could be no barrier to being united in marriage, just to get the benefits and respect of the institution of marriage.

In order to make same-sex couples feel more normal and affirmed, the government is ignoring other more natural and perhaps more loving unions, such as heterosexual sisters or brothers living together and same-sex heterosexual roommates. **Our tendency today, and if we allow it even more so in the future, is to cater to the loudest minorities with a show of tolerance that may be comforting but is very selective and unfair.**

Not only has God established marriage as between a man and a woman, but also in the Old Testament, He consistently has described Israel (now the church) as being the bride of God (Jesus). (See Isaiah 54:5–6 and Hosea 2:19–20.) Likewise in the New Testament, Jesus is the bridegroom and the church is the bride. This concept is even carried into heaven as described in Revelation. A same-sex couple destroys the Bible's concept of Jesus being the husband and the church being the wife, as a complete family, and the government has no right to force the abuse of a biblical covenant.

SEXUAL VARIANTS

In this section I am discussing those people who classify themselves as something other than heterosexual. The word "variants" is not intended to be derogatory but to mean *different*. To some, that classification applies to gender, to others it signifies their preference for having sexual relations. The current popular acronym is LGBT, lesbian, gay, bisexual, transgender. God has, through His Creation, minimized sexual variants through marriage between a man and a woman, but the government has stolen and redefined God's plan for marriage. The simple reason for God's original plan was for his children to "be fruitful and multiply and fill the earth and subdue it" (Genesis 1:28). Other relationships should certainly be allowed but should not be called marriage, since that was, and is, exclusively God's plan.

The push for transgender acceptance is another step in the "since I am God, I have the right to redesign myself" movement. It began with the feminine tendency of bodily decoration such as tattoos (prohibited in Leviticus 19:28), and it has proceeded to sex change ("male and female He created them"). When we are dissatisfied with the way God has created us, we think we can just improve His "unthoughtful" work through our superior wisdom and aesthetics.

Not only is marriage, as defined by God, biblical, but the union between the sexes is also demonstrated by nature. **A species would become extinct without union between the sexes. It is interesting that many who promote alternate marriages are panicked about the loss of a species in the animal kingdom.** Since the primary purpose of marriage is procreation of God's children, again we see a parallel in nature. This natural attraction (in types of animals and in people) is demonstrated through the way animals form herds, flocks, and schools exclusively within their species. Jude 1:7 says, "Just as Sodom and Gomorrah and the surrounding cities, which likewise indulged in sexual immorality and pursued *unnatural* desire, serve an example by undergoing a punishment of eternal fire."

All of the variants mentioned involve homosexuality, which is not natural in the animal kingdom, as explained above. Likewise, homosexuality is not biblically designed. Beginning in Genesis 1:27 the Bible explains, "So God created man in His own image, in the image of God He created him; male and female He created them." This design and differentiation concerning marriage is further described in more detail in

Genesis 2:18, 22,23,24; Matthew 19:4–6; Mark 10:6–8; Romans 1:23–27; and 1 Corinthians 6:9. Homosexual relations are prohibited in accordance with these marital standards in Leviticus 18:22, 20:13; Romans 1:26–27; 1 Corinthians 6:9; and 1 Timothy 1:10.

There are three possibilities a person is homosexual: choice, God's plan, or experience.

The argument that there is a gay gene was promoted in a 1993 study that reported that some male homosexuals who were related through a maternal line—such as gay sons with gay uncles on their mother's side—shared some similarities within a large DNA region on the X chromosome. A 2014 analysis of a larger group of test subjects found a similar link, but the similar sequences did not include a gene nor did the research support the conclusion that any DNA directly or indirectly determines sexuality.[1] So DNA, according to these results, does not determine or cause homosexual behavior. Michael Bailey, the senior author of this study, said that there are certainly other environmental factors involved.

There will obviously be DNA similarities in people who are kin, but homosexual behavior seems to be caused exclusively by environmental contact between individuals—most often between those in the same extended family, probably because of closer exposure.

There is a great deal of controversy today about whether these alternative lifestyles promote child abuse in marriage, education, or recreation. It could be argued that the risk of young girls or boys being abused by heterosexual authority figures is the same as the risk of being abused by homosexuals, or that the heterosexual risk is even greater since there are many more heterosexual authority figures. But since a complete education must involve both ages and both sexes exposed to each other, educational administrators must assure that the relationships are not abused in either case. There is potentially no more traumatic event in a child's life than forced, or even consensual, sex before the age of rational choice. As I have mentioned before, a young person's cognitive ability is not fully developed before about twenty-five years of age on average.

To prevent abuse, administrators should insist that—outside of the family—no school teacher, coach, Sunday School teacher, youth-group leader, camp counselor, or Scout leader be alone with a child without other people nearby and doors open. That is not an unreasonable or unfair requirement, and if it is opposed, the opposition should be rigorously questioned as to their motives. It is worth the sacrifice of freedom for a few to protect our children. A person who has a tendency toward pederasty or hebephilia (attraction for the young) should be removed from the temptation. It appears that the vast majority of homosexuals are not tempted in this way, just as the vast majority of heterosexuals are not so tempted.

The most serious studies indicate that heterosexuals of both sexes are more likely to molest children below eleven years of age (pederasts), and homosexuals are more likely to molest minors between eleven and fourteen (hebephiles). There is some professional disagreement in this, but it is mostly semantic. This is another example of how out-of-context statistics can be used to argue any point. But the main caution for the future is to remove the temptation from anyone who uses children sexually. A loving person, regardless of sexual preferences, will never abuse a child—especially his own.

Homosexual people must be accepted and loved for who they are. God made them, and God has allowed them to be what they are. We can't question God in this issue. Their proclivity may be unnatural but so are the tendencies of many so-called normal people. No one is really normal; normal is just average. Everyone is literally above or below normal, and it is therefore unreasonable and unjust to ostracize a person who is different. Each of us, in this life, is but a flawed image bearer of God.

We must invite homosexuals into our churches and watch God either change them or allow them to be sexually inactive or monogamous. Homosexuals, as many minorities, may have been mistreated in the past, and we need to mature past those primitive actions and treat them as fallen equals.

One of the unspoken questions in this issue is why these marital issues have to be about sex instead of love. Does love require sex? Are we prone to favor same-sex marriage in order to legitimize same-sex intercourse or for benefits? If the real purpose is to legitimize sex acts, where does this tolerance take us in the future? There is a purpose of a sexual act—both natural and God-given—and that is procreation with pleasure: pleasure in order to promote procreation. This purpose has nothing to do with civil union or marriage benefits or even freedom. Same-sex marriage is much like other Supreme Court legislation: the right to murder living fetuses for the convenience of the mother. That legislation legalized murder; now we have legitimatized sex for pleasure alone, not for procreation as intended. Again, what follows for the future? Sex with children, sex with the dead, slavery and trafficking of minors in order to enjoy sex. If the real issue is respectable sex, why not? If legalization makes any type of sex or murder legal, what keeps us from going there in order to feel more tolerant and get a few more votes?

Beware; media is already in panic mode to promote aberrant sex as normal, and government is following the media as an unthinking puppy.

Perhaps the most dangerous practice of a minority of homosexuals today is the concerted organizational efforts of groups like NAMBLA (North American Man-Boy Love Association) and others less overt, such as Gay Straight Alliances, to encourage young children to "come out." The result of this blatant effort in communities and in schools is pressure on children to feel that they are a homosexual, even if they only have normal adolescent sexual feelings and are ripe for experimentation. It seems that it is not abnormal for children to have some same sex attraction, that are either nonsexual and healthy, or experimentally sexual without lust. These occasional attractions can be with the same or with the opposite sex, but they do not mean that a child should "come out" and commit to such a lifestyle. The tempter in these instances usually has a goal of increasing those of his kind in order to make himself feel more normal and accepted. This is perhaps the most evil sexually related trend going forward into our future: to encourage—or force—by so-called kindness and sympathy, a young, immature person to accept a lifestyle as normal for him or herself, when the person is only curious.

Divorce

The other destructive force in marriage today is divorce. God hates divorce. (See Matthew 5:32, 19:3–9; Malachi 2:14; Mark 10:11–12; Luke 16:18; and 1 Corinthians 7:12–15.) It is clear that His plan for the human race was a lifelong marriage without adultery. Some churches increasingly permit member divorce in the case of unfaithfulness, sexual immorality, an unbelieving spouse, physical abuse, verbal abuse, lack of emotional support, abandonment, or even emotional abandonment. These rationalizations, as in many interpretations of the Bible, take the inspired words and re-define them to meet a permissive goal of sinlessness. The trend of Christian and non-Christian divorces is going up; therefore, to preserve the institution of marriage in the future, this trend must stop. At risk are children, families, the couple, and the church itself.

Secular society cannot be depended on to reverse this trend, especially due to its belief in evolution. After all, they may figure, animals never marry, and we are descended from them. **Therefore it is up to Christian and Jewish churches to teach the rest of the world the origin of marriage and the requirements to preserve the institution.**

Families

The Bible and secular authorities concur[2] that the ideal setting for raising stable children is in a marriage, with one male and one female parent. In a recent Pew Research report[3], 77 percent of those polled said that it is esier for a married person than a single person to raise a family.So the preservation of the historical family structure is the answer to the future stability of species. In order to assure this future, those who accept God's Word as true and final must stand tall and speak clearly. The future of species is in God's hand, but we can improve the interim future by allowing Him to work through each of us. When secular law is in conflict with God's law, a Christian may decide to peacefully disobey the secular law in protest or to at least speak out strongly in protest. **The church has failed so far in its opposition to the murder of the unborn and its support of marriage, and it must do a better job in this case of the destruction of families if the future is to be civilized.**

---

1 Brian Thomas, *Does DNA Determine Sexual Preference? Acts & Facts*, June 2015.17
2 Yongminn Son and Yoanzhang Li, *Journal of Marriage and Family*, Ohio State University,2011, Abstract accessed October 12,2015; Terry-Ann Craigic, Princeton U., Jeanne Brooks- Gunn, Columbia U., Jane Waldfogel, Columbia U, *Family Structure, Family Stability and Early Childhood Wellbeing.* (Contains scores of appropriate references). Accessed October 12,2015.
3 Pew Research Center, *Love and Marriage*, 2013, accessed October 12,2015.

CHAPTER 42
The Future of Health Care

I am content in my later years. I have kept my good humor and take neither myself nor the next person seriously. Albert Einstein, 1950, 53

HEALTH CARE, LIKE WEALTH AND position, is not considered a right in the Constitution. A few years ago, the cost of health care had risen to the point that its expenses were one of the highest for a family—higher in many cases than the necessities of food, clothing, or shelter. An additional concern arose when health-care insurance was denied for those with pre-existing conditions. Hospitals were charging thousands of dollars a day for a room, medical doctors were doubling up on their services, and prescription and insurance costs were rising uncontrolled.

The government tried to resolve the issues—which are not in the realm of government responsibility—by proposed legislation regulating hospitals, medical, and pharmaceutical charges, and insurance. This initial overreach of the government was defeated in the late 1990s but was passed into law in the form of the Affordable Care Act in 2010. The implementation of this Act has resolved the insurance issue of excluding preconditions and has provided insurance for thousands of uninsured people, but it has caused many hospitals and medical practitioners to go out of business. The law is now under review to retain the positive provisions and eliminate those that are damaging or impractical.

It appears that the future will have serious challenges as the population becomes older due to past health-care improvements and innovations. Survival will require a consensus on whether health care and health insurance are entitlements and, if so, the method of financing these benefits without losing quality and efficiency. If employers are required to provide minimal insurance, what will be included? What about self-imposed—as opposed to doctor-prescribed costs such as for abortions, drug-, alcohol-, and tobacco-abuse treatment, preventive medicine, vitamins, natural remedies, alternative medicine, cannabis treatment, and more? Will the public be responsible to subsidize treatment for these growing self-imposed practices and addictions? Who is qualified to prescribe medication and treatment?

The future of medical care will require wisdom beyond that of politicians, in order to resolve these critical issues with fairness and compassion.

CHAPTER 43
The Future of Social Life

*Yes, my girlfriends and sailboat remained in Berlin.
But Hitler only wanted the latter, which was insulting
to the former. Albert Einstein, about 1935, 83*

MOST PEOPLE ARE TO SOME degree social, just as animals naturally are. There are several ways of relating socially to others, primarily with our five senses: sight, hearing, taste, smell, and touch. The more senses that can be incorporated, the closer the social relationship becomes.

With recent technology applied to social media, the initiation of relationships has changed, but the implementation of those relationships can only progress personally, through the senses. Social life includes interaction in jobs, social events, and also through leisure-time activities and hobbies such as sports, recreation, games, study groups, discussion groups, church, and civic activities. Fellowship has been important throughout history because of the trust that it develops between people, and this will continue into the future.

Technology will also affect our freedom, since freedom and security many times are in conflict. If the government is allowed to continue to take more control of our lives, we can expect freedom to diminish. Already the Global Positioning System (GPS) navigation technology, along with increased cell-phone use, gives governments and others the potential ability to track everyone twenty-four hours a day. This capability can be justified by arguing that it could increase safety and security, but the potential for abuse seems to be much greater than any benefit to society. Another potentially abusive trend is that credit-card records allow the characterization of citizens based on purchases.

Many people today allow their emotions and their perceived emotional well-being to quench their intelligence. They live for the highs of their past or the imagined highs of their future. According to John Shinal in an article in *USA Today*, published July 19, 2015, as "drug use becomes more passé than avant gard" and "as meditative yoga and organized religion jostle for popularity among spiritually minded Americans," new electronic "devices that instantly and reliably deliver altered states of mind in social settings" are offered "to entice the young to tune in and work harder, as dropping out is no longer an economic option." This is simply a nondrug-induced stimuli to replace the burden and effort of deep thought and fellowship.

So technology and government control will change our social lives and our professional or job lives. It is our responsibility to assure that this change is positive. It is also our responsibility to insist that social opportunities remain available in order to promote communication, friendship, and trust in our communities.

CHAPTER 44
The Future of Retirement

I have to apologize to you that I am still among the living. There will be a remedy for this, however. Albert Einstein, 1946, 13

OLDER PEOPLE AND SOME WHO are younger are interested in retiring at some point. For many, that is the American dream. The federal Social Security system, Individual Retirement

Accounts, a large portion of union dues, and many employment benefits are designed around gradually paying into a fund—usually tax free—and receiving the payments plus interest and/or dividends, upon reaching retirement age. Many companies, as well as most governments, set an age, usually sixty-five, when an employee must retire. This leaves room for younger, lower-paid employees to take the places of retirees but forces a brain drain on society.

The question should be asked as to whether that system will be feasible in the future. We hear that the Social Security system is going broke and that many seniors cannot afford to quit work.

There seems to be no guidance in the Bible about retirement or any encouragement to ever quit working. But the elders in ancient cities did seem to spend a lot of time sitting around the city gates. In Proverbs and in Paul's writings to Timothy and Titus, there is much about the responsibilities of older men and women to teach the younger and for the younger to show respect.

This seems to indicate that retirement should be optional. If people want to work exceptionally hard in order to rest in their twilight years, and if they will use this rest as the Sabbath-day rest of Creation—to worship, serve, and glorify God—then the retiree will certainly please God.

There is a biblical responsibility for children and other family members to provide for their relatives and especially for members of their household (1 Timothy 5:4 and 8). There is also an obligation for churches to care for older widows. (See 1 Timothy 5:9 and also the book of Acts.)

Parents have a biblical responsibility to their children and grandchildren all of their lives. Living apart from them may not honor this responsibility. Others who have no children or grandchildren have no such obligation and are free to minister wherever they are. As is made clear, especially in Proverbs, each person's situation is different, as is their relation to God, and we are free to serve Him in our own way as long as He is first.

It would be a shame for us to miss the opportunity of influencing our grandchildren. So often, raising children is a tyranny of the urgent. We want to protect them and keep them out of trouble, and we often don't take the time to train them up as they should go. If retired grandparents can influence their grandchildren in a loving way that is not manipulative, there could be no better use of retirement, and they will certainly be pleasing God.

So retirement can be a wonderful time in the future if we retain the right to keep our hard-earned money in order to cover our expenses. It can provide a well-deserved rest, but more than that, it can give us the time and opportunities to serve God in new and different ways. There should be no governmental limits that restrict or limit heath care because of life expectancy.

It is of critical importance to future society that we provide a means of transferring the wisdom of the aged to younger members

of society. There are many older people who have acquired real wisdom over the years, and that wisdom is no less valuable than what we read in history books. Why would we spend hours studying from the latest guru, when we can probably get better personal, business, and spiritual advice from someone who really loves us, for free?

CHAPTER 45
The Future of the Church

I consider the Society of Friends the religious community that has the highest moral standards. As far as I know, they have never made evil compromises and are always guided by their conscience. In international life, especially, their influence seems to me very beneficial and effective. Albert Einstein, 1954, 207

JESUS CHRIST ESTABLISHED THE CHURCH as His bride (2 Corinthians 11:2). Ephesians 5:25–27 says, "Husbands, love your wives, as Christ loved the church and gave Himself up for her, that He might sanctify her, having cleansed her by the washing of water with the Word, so that He might present the church to Himself in splendor, without spot or wrinkle or any such thing, that she might be holy and without blemish." This concept of being married to God began in the Old Testament view of Israel (now the church). (See Isaiah 54:5 and 62:4–5.)

In the future the church must continue to be a "pillar and buttress of the truth" (1 Timothy 3:15), since it was purchased with Jesus's blood (Acts 20:28). God gave us Jesus "as head over all things to the church, which is His body, the fullness of Him Who fills all in all" (Ephesians 1:22–23).

The Bible directs the church to be undivided (Romans 16:17, 1 Corinthians 1:10), to teach, admonish, and praise (Acts 5:42, 20:20, Ephesians 3:10, Colossians 3:16), to love and help each other (1 John 3:14–17), and to send out missionaries (Acts 13:2–4). Many churches do not like to hear it, but the main responsibility of the church—as taught in both the Old and New Testaments—is to teach the Bible, and the main responsibility of the members is "to praise God and enjoy Him forever" (Westminster Confession of Faith). **Many times it is easier for a church to fellowship and pastor—both good things—than to accurately exposit God's Word. (That could run people off.) It is easier for a member to act as a missionary than to truly worship.**

Some of the more instructive and interesting verses concerning churches are in Revelation 2 and 3:

- Ephesus, good—hard work, patient endurance, tested and cannot bear evil and false people, hate works of evil
- Ephesus, bad—abandoned first love
- Smyrna, good—suffered tribulation, poverty, and slander, spiritually rich
- Smyrna, bad—nothing
- Pergamum, good—hold fast Jesus's name, do not deny their faith
- Pergamum, bad—some hold to false teaching
- Thyatira, good—love, faith, service, patient endurance, growing works
- Thyatira, bad—some tolerate false prophets
- Sardis, good—some have not soiled their garments due to cosistant obedience and courageous faith
- Sardis, bad—dead, incomplete works
- Philadelphia, good—have an open door, only have little power, kept Jesus's word about patient endurance, do not deny Jesus's name
- Philadelphia, bad—nothing
- Laodicea, good—nothing
- Laodicea, bad—lukewarm, wretched, pitiable, poor, blind, naked

The all-good churches—Smyrna and Philadelphia—were naturally poor, powerless, and persecuted, but spiritually rich; they were doctrinally faithful, and did not dilute God's Word.

The bad churches—Laodicea and Sardis—were dead of works, except for a few, blind of spirit, and lukewarm. Jesus's judgment is not exactly what we would use today to judge contemporary churches that will be successful in the future. Jesus didn't care about church wealth and membership; he cared about faithfulness, keeping God's Word, and spiritual life.

Note that even in the case of Sardis and Laodicea, Jesus commended them for the few faithful and warned them to wake up before it was too late (Sardis). He also counseled Laodicea in love, reproof, and discipline. Jesus never gives up; only we do that.

In the future the church will survive—God promises it—but it could well be much smaller and less biblical than it is now. This is demonstrated by the decline of the church in Europe and by the declining membership of the mainline churches in the United States. Other than the failure to preach the complete Gospel (Bible), how else can the fall of theologically liberal churches and the rise of theologically conservative churches be explained? Also, the more biblically faithful churches of South America, Africa, and China are continuing to grow.

I believe that our interim future quality of life is dependent on our churches following their biblical purpose and resisting the temptation to grow at the expense of teaching the truth.

CHAPTER 46

Conclusion

§

If one purges all subsequent additions from the original teachings of the Prophets and Christianity, especially those of the priests, one is left with a doctrine that is capable of curing all the social ills of humankind. Albert Einstein, 1933, 200

WE LIVE IN A WORLD containing much communication urging us to become independent from God and justifying narcissistic behavior as independence. Darwin's *The Origin of Species* accelerated the flight from the truth of the Bible, has been extrapolated to mean more than its intention, and has caused generations of children to believe lies about their origin and their accountability. The big advantage to individuals in ignoring God is that they think that they can find themselves, be completely independent, make their own rules, and blame all problems on others. The godless advantage to scientists is that they can believe that they can understand and control everything and that there is no outside, uncontrollable force interfering. The advantage to our rulers is that we are easier to control if they make the laws rather than a distant god. So the "Me" generation teaches their children and our children how good it feels to be free of the bondage of God, and the millennial generation demands entitlement and instant gratification.

Many young people today consider themselves spiritual but not religious, and the Holy Spirit is certainly not limited to acting in churchgoing people. But Jesus left the church in His stead (Ephesians 1:23) and purchased it with His own blood (Acts 20:28). So the decline in attendees in Christian churches is discouraging, but the rise in attendance in Bible-teaching Christian churches is very encouraging. Many modern churches have eliminated *offensive* Bible teaching in order to attract more young *seekers* without risking rejection. **But the weakened entertainment that has replaced God's Word lacks the power of the actual words of God, and the seekers are not fooled.**

The results of the decline of our churches and the anti-God movement is obvious, if not admitted: more crime by the young, more terrorism in the name of religion, more unstable and nonexistent families and parents, more poverty, more wars, more minds destroyed by drugs, and less scientific advancement, less educational excellence, and fewer great scientists, artists, and politicians.

Our future cries for a movement to truth as defined by God in the Bible. Without the understanding and practice of this truth, civilization will continue to devolve through independence, selfishness, riot, and revolution into an uncontrolled and uncontrollable tribal system ruled by the criminally wealthy for their own benefit.

If we will accept the only true knowledge, we can be removed from—or coexist with—the disasters, plagues, and evil that are predicted in the Book of Revelation, and we can realize the future of truth that God has planned for His children, as also described in Revelation.

As preparation for the future, money, wealth, and freedom are all good things—and those who possess them should share—but the most lasting gift is simply sharing the words of Jesus, which is the entire Bible. Then all will be "storing up treasure for themselves as a good foundation for the future, so that they may take hold of that which is truly life" (1 Timothy 6:19).

In order to understand and accept the reality of the past, present and future, we must explore and answer the elemental but .difficult questions of life presented in chapter 2. These deep and important questions must begin with the huge issue of whether only natural reality exists, as descibed in chapter 4 or whether there is a supernatural or spiritual reality, as described in chapter 5. If the later is true, since we are natural beings, there can be no communication with or understanding of a supernatural reality, without that communication being unilateral from the spiritual to the natural. As explained in chapter 6, Christians and jews believe that a supernatural communication has occurred in the form of the Old Testament of the Holy Bible, and Christians believe that a supernatural communication has occurred again in the form of the New Testament of the Holy Bible. **The Messiah of the Old Testament, known as Jesus in the New Testament, is called the Word, since both Testaments agree that He was present during Creation and inspired the original writings of both Testaments.**

Using these logical beliefa as a basis for understanding reality, I propose the following as a conclusion to this analysis of the past, present and future of species;

- **The supernatural reality is a separate dimension from natural reality and has infinite size, power, wisdom and control over the natural reality that it created. It has no limitations from a natural or supernatural perspective, or it would not be infinate.**
- Within this supernatural reality, the created natural reality has finite power, wisdom and limitations within the three dimensions of length, width and depth, and a forth dimension of time.
- **The supernatural reality, having no constaint of time, is able to see and know the past, present and future of the natural reality, concurrently.**
- During Old Testament times, God permeated natural reality in the form of Creation, other miracles, the Prophets, and the written Word in the form of the Old Testament.
- In spite of efforts through the ages to change the accepted dating method, time in natural reality has remained split into before Christ, and after Christ. This practice reflects the truth of the historical event of Jesus of the Trinitarian God, entering the natural world from the supernatural.

- **For the approximately thirty years of Jesus' life, God permeated natural reality in the form of Jesus' birth, teachings, miracles, death and resurrection.**
- When Jesus was murdered for His innocence and truthfulness, and rose out of the natural reality to be back with His Father in the spitiual reality, He sent the Holy Spirit of the Trinitarian God in His place to spiritually live within the natural bodies of those who love God and are called according to His purpose (Romans 8:28).
- **This death of Jesus and resultant death of Satan and sin, was planned by the Trinity before the Creation. Jesus willingly subjected Himself to the ridicule, torture and death from mankind in His obedience to His Father and His love for that mankind. How amazing and exciting!**
- From thirty to about sixty years after Jesus' death, God permeated natural reality through the books of the written Word in the form of the New Testament.
- Since the New Testament was completed, God's revelation to His Created humans has enabled a much better understanding of His truth as expressed in both Testaments of the Scriptures, through a Helper in the form of the Holy Spirit to enable us to interpret those Scripures in a way that was impossible before that Helper came into God's people at Pentecost. That Holy Spirit continues, as it did the Godly people of the Old Testament, to allow bilateral communication directly to God.
- Today, each person in this world, outside of the travesty of slavery, owns at least their own bodies, an ownership given to us by God at Creation, which cannot be removed. As owners we have the complete responsibility for the mental, physical and spiritual health of those bodies. Christians have an even more critical responsibility, since their bodies are the temple of the supernatural God, in the form of the Holy Spirit.
- The critical truth and importance of the indwelling Holy Spirit is that our natural tendency toward sin will be overcome when God regenerates us by putting into us a completely new disposition in

the form of the Holy Spirit, that enables us to lead a completely new responsible moral life.
- **Through this supernatural process God has linked the supernatural and the natural unilaterally to allow us to learn God's mysteries and through prayer, actually see our lives and the lives of others changed. This miracle from God demonstrates the exclusively Christian concept of the answer for *sin* (out heredity, our tendency), as opposed to other religions' answer only for our *sins*.(our specific actions).**

So imagine, if you can, an infinate supernatural reality (occupied only by the holy Trinity), containing a finite natural reality, which was created by and is controlled by, the supernatural reality. Then imagine a link (in the form of Jesus Christ), between the realities, caused, as it only could be, by the Supernatural reality through love and grace, allowing a new understanding of, and better communication between, the two realities (because of the continued link, the Holy Spirit). The miraculous extent of that link is, for the first time in history, the actual spiritual presence of God within our bodies. How exciting is that!

So today, if you are concerned about the future of species and interested in experiencing peace and satisfaction with yourself and in others, I recommend that you consider the following:

- **Decide whether there is any supernatural existence of any kind.**
- Ask what that existence is and how it is controlled.
- Ask whether that spiritual reality is in control of, or controlled by, natural reality.
- Ask whether it is random or organized—and if organized, by whom.
- **If you admit that the organizer could be called God, how powerful is He?**
- **If He has limitations, who or what limits Him?**

- If you can reach the point where you admit that God, by definition, is unlimited, submit yourself to that God, with an understanding that He can do anything He wishes, since His position as head of supernatural reality is in complete control of you and all natural things. **This submission to God and His Son Jesus—Who He sent as God to this world to teach us His Way and to be sacrificed and punished as a payment for our sins, present, past, and future—qualifies you for adoption as God's child.**
- As a child you have, for the first time, the right to communicate with a Holy God through prayer, and as a Father, He has elected to hear and answer your prayers and, through His Word, to teach you how to be one, as a son or daughter, with God your Father.
- Admit, if you can, that God is good, not bad, and therefore cannot lie or deceive.
- **Admit that this good God is a God of love, not hate, and with His infinite power, He has infinite, complete, and perfect love for you and will forgive all of your sins through the sacrifice of His Son Jesus.**
- Admit that a God of infinite love and power will, in His love, communicate with His children, with perfect and easily understandable words.
- Admit that since God selected the written word for that communication, He—in His love and power—has caused that Word to be supernaturally without error and to be believable in its accurate translations.
- Immerse yourself with prayer in God's Word as expressed in the Holy Bible and the expositional teaching of that Word.
- **And, above all, believe in Jesus Christ. Believe with a faith, a trust, a passion, as you've never believed before, and just sit back, watch, and enjoy as God transforms you into oneness with Him.**

This should not be difficult, even for a cynic, since if you accept what both the Bible and contemporary secular writings say about

The Future of Species

Jesus, He had to be—in the words of Josh McDowell—a liar, a lunatic, or the Lord. There remains no other option.

For those of us who will accept God's promises, He says in 1 John 5:4–5, "For everyone who has been born of God overcomes the world. And this is the victory that has overcome the world—our faith. Who is it that overcomes the world except the one who believes that Jesus is the Son of God?"

Oneness with God will allow us to overcome the pressures and evil of the future world by our love, belief, and faith. We will not keep on sinning, regardless of what everyone else does, and thus we will be changed, along with our family and our loved ones. 1 John 5:18–19 explains it this way: "We know that everyone who has been born of God does not keep on sinning, but He Who was born of God protects him, and the evil one does not touch him. We know that we are from God, and the whole world lies in the power of the evil one."

Your new self will feel the love and grace of God, will find a new love for others, will be privileged to serve others, will be delighted to share your newfound freedom from the yoke of sin, and will realize a new joy in worshiping and living to please God.

I believe that if you do these things—not as a formula but as principles—you will have absolute assurance that you are a child of God, eligible for all of His love and peace, and that you will feel that love and peace constantly grow in His enjoyment and service. And then you will have no concerns about the future of species.

Yes, folks, there was a big bang, but it was not as we are told. Instead it was the explosion of the supernatural God entering the natural world as Jesus and changing the history—present and future—of species!

That future is in God's hands, not ours, but we are called as His instruments. Praise His Holy Name!

Acknowledgments

I MUST GIVE MY DEEPEST thanks to the following friends who read, checked, edited, and/or suggested additions and improvements to *The Future of Species*. Their help was invaluable as peer review and to make the manuscript more readable.

- E. Roberts Alley, Jr., President, Elrod & Company, LLC, Engineering Consultants
- Mark Anderson, Chair, Department of Philosophy, Director of Classics, Author, Belmont University
- R. E. Speece, Centennial Professor Emeritus of Environmental Engineering, Vanderbilt University
- Larry Stone, Author, Publishing Consultant, Kingsley Books, Inc.

About the Author

E. ROBERTS ALLEY IS A registered professional engineer and has practiced and taught environmental engineering for over fifty years, working primarily for industrial and municipal clients to lower their residual discharges to the environment. He holds a bachelor's of engineering degree and a master's of science degree from Vanderbilt University.

Bob is chairman of the board of E. Roberts Alley & Associates, Inc. and New Era Holdings, Inc. He has taught environmental courses at Vanderbilt University, the University of Tennessee, East Tennessee State University, George Washington University, The Centre for Management Technology, and several other universities and organizations in the United States, England, France, Singapore, Malaysia, and Indonesia.

He has been an elder in two Presbyterian (PCA) churches and a deacon in one of them and has taught youth and adult Sunday school for thirty years. Bob was a scoutmaster for twenty years and has four wonderful children and ten amazing grandchildren.

Bob grew up and lives in Nashville, Tennessee.

Books by E. Roberts Alley

Routine Quantitative Test for Salmonella Organisms in Natural Waters, Environmental and Water Resources Engineering, Vanderbilt University, 1973.
Drainage Management, University of Tennessee Center for Government Training, 1991.
Air Quality Control Handbook, McGraw-Hill, 1998.
Water Quality Control Handbook, McGraw-Hill, 2000.
Manual de Control de la Calidad del Aire, McGraw-Hill, 2001.
Water Quality Control Handbook, Second Edition, McGraw-Hill, 2007.
A Christian Environmentalist, Xulon Press, 2013.

Made in the USA
Charleston, SC
28 November 2015